Mothers on
the Fast Track

Mothers on
the Fast Track

How a New Generation

Can Balance Family and Careers

MARY ANN MASON
EVE MASON EKMAN

OXFORD
UNIVERSITY PRESS

2007

OXFORD
UNIVERSITY PRESS

Oxford University Press, Inc., publishes works that further
Oxford University's objective of excellence
in research, scholarship, and education.

Oxford   New York
Auckland   Cape Town   Dar es Salaam   Hong Kong   Karachi
Kuala Lumpur   Madrid   Melbourne   Mexico City   Nairobi
New Delhi   Shanghai   Taipei   Toronto

With offices in
Argentina   Austria   Brazil   Chile   Czech Republic   France   Greece
Guatemala   Hungary   Italy   Japan   Poland   Portugal   Singapore
South Korea   Switzerland   Thailand   Turkey   Ukraine   Vietnam

Copyright © 2007 by Mary Ann Mason and Eve Mason Ekman

Published by Oxford University Press, Inc.
198 Madison Avenue, New York, NY 10016

www.oup.com

Library of Congress Cataloging-in-Publication Data
Mason, Mary Ann.
Mothers on the fast track : how a new generation can balance family
and careers / Mary Ann Mason and Eve Mason Ekman.
    p. cm.
Includes bibliographical references and index.
ISBN 978–0–19–518267–5 (hardcover)   1. Working mothers—United States—Case studies.
2. Mothers—Employment—United States—Case studies.   3. Work and
family—United States—Case studies.   I. Ekman, Eve Mason.   II. Title.
HQ759.48M347 2007
306.874'3097309045—dc22   2006100026

9 8 7 6 5 4 3 2 1

Printed in the United States of America
on acid-free paper

CONTENTS

ACKNOWLEDGMENTS

Eve and I would like to thank the scores of women and men, only a fraction of whose words appear in the book, who contributed their ideas and stories about this critically important topic. Friends and colleagues in many settings—large audiences at my research talks, fellow students and colleagues in Eve's world—have been generous and open. I would particularly like to thank all my graduate students, who every day remind me why this life issue is so important to them.

My research associate Marc Goulden, the co-investigator of our Do Babies Matter? project, provided the indispensable research base that underlies all the arguments in this book; he deserves special thanks. The rest of our team—Angie Stacy, Karie Frasch, Nick Wolfinger, Carol Hoffman, and Sharon Page-Medrich—helped with both the research and the implementation of new policies, the UC Faculty Family Friendly Edge initiatives, which have generated national attention and are beginning to change the culture.

Much of this good work was enabled by generous grants from the Alfred P. Sloan Foundation, whose program director, Kathleen Christiansen, has been a guiding light in the work–family field nationally.

On the editorial side, Korey Capozza, a graduate student in public health with a strong journalism background, has helped shape and refine the arguments and integrate the interviews with the research. We are most grateful for her hard work and great insights. Sharon Page-Medrich, my assistant, also helped a great deal with the editorial process.

Other students and colleagues have contributed in many ways. Rena Scott, now a practicing lawyer, helped with background research on the many fields we covered. My faculty colleagues in the Berkeley Family Forum who regularly meet and collaborate in writing books on family policy have all been supportive and inspirational and have dealt with parts of the draft at various times. Special thanks among them go to Neil Gilbert, Paula Fass, Steve

Sugarman, Joan Williams, Jill Duerr Berrick, Joan Hollinger, and Arlene Skolnick.

My husband—Eve's father—Paul Ekman has been a partner, supporter, and sharp editorial critic at every step of the way. This has truly been a family endeavor, with Tom, our son, a wonderful sounding board for our ideas.

Introduction

Do Babies Matter? Mothers on the Fast Track

"It's 51 percent!" exclaimed my assistant Judi, thrusting new registration figures before my eyes. "Women are 51 percent of our new graduate student class. This makes history!"

This was the year 2000. I had just become the first woman graduate dean at the University of California, Berkeley. Berkeley confers more doctorates than any other university in the country, and the university's eleven professional graduate schools cover almost all professions, from law to public health to journalism to business administration. There are nearly 10,000 students in all.

As I greeted this incoming class of 2,500 new graduate students, more than half of whom were women, I realized that this was a moment anticipated by the women of my generation who had struggled to open the gates to high-status, male-dominated occupations. Achieving graduate degrees, we believed, would lead to professional and economic equality. We hoped that once a critical mass of women entered the "fast track," the power balance between men and women would inevitably be achieved in boardrooms, courtrooms, and university classrooms.

I was excited and proud when I announced this historic first to the evenly mixed audience of young graduate men and women. But soon my enthusiasm was tempered by a familiar reality check at a faculty senate meeting that same afternoon. Looking around the chamber, I saw only a few female faces. As a longtime faculty member, I was accustomed to this dynamic; at Berkeley, only 23 percent of the tenure-track faculty are women, a number that has been stagnant for about a decade. This is not simply a chronological lag. Last spring, women received 46 percent of the doctorates granted at Berkeley, but this fall only 26 percent of the new faculty hires on campus were women. This hiring-gap of nearly two to one has been the norm for four decades.[1]

Women are even less visible in the administrative power structure. At the first meeting of deans I attended that fall of 2000, I stood out as the only woman at the conference table. "You're in a box by yourself," the dean next to me commented, studying the organizational chart of deans. Alas, it was true. Equal student participation in graduate studies is a step forward, but it's too early to declare victory in academia.

The imbalance between gender equity at the beginning of the race toward career success and male dominance at the finish is still the norm in the university world. In fact, it's also the norm in law, medicine, and the corporate world. The number of women sitting at a senior partners' meeting in a major law firm, a chiefs' meeting in a university hospital, or the top executive conference in a Fortune 500 firm would look very much like our deans' meeting.

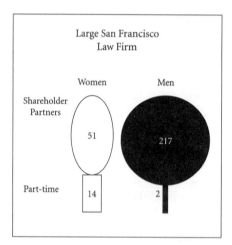

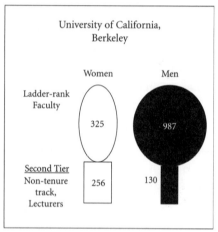

These two trends—women entering graduate and professional schools in record numbers and fewer reaching the top of their professions—raise important questions. What happens between school and the boardroom that causes large numbers of women to drop off of this fast track? When does the exit start to occur? And what solutions will stem this retreat? Can mothers remain on the fast track? And if so, what is the secret to their success?

In this book we will address such questions by applying our research on careers and family over the life course. We will both frame the issues and offer solutions. The qualitative component of our research—interviews with dozens of women pursuing or sidetracked from fast track careers—tells the story of how these issues play out in women's lives. Drawing on both their advice and our research, we will offer personal and institutional strategies for helping women succeed as professionals, wives, and parents.

The idea for this book came in part from my women graduate students who frequently ask, When is a good time to have a baby? While this question seems straightforward, there are no easy answers and few studies have tackled this question. We know more about why women don't succeed than about how they do. Arlie Hochschild in *The Second Shift* shows that, in spite of women's massive entry into full-time employment, they still bear the burden of family care at home.[2] Ann Crittenden, in *The Wages of Motherhood*, argues that working mothers lose out on all economic fronts in large part because our society doesn't value motherhood.[3] And Joan Williams in *Unbending Gender* observes that the inflexible "ideal worker" model of the American workplace discriminates against mothers, undermining the purpose of Title VII.[4] When I examined these issues in my earlier book, *The Equality Trap*, I suggested that opening the door to women without changing the structure of the workplace was setting up mothers for failure.[5]

Some women, however, do manage to have it all, juggling family and fast-paced careers. When do women who stay on the fast track have their children? When do their careers take off? Studies to date have counted the heads of women who have succeeded in a particular profession, but they have not systematically tracked women over their career span. There is little understanding of why some women succeed or what happens to women who drop out. Perhaps only now, a full generation after the major entrance of women into male-dominated professions, can we begin to see clearly how the story of women on the fast track unfolds from university education to retirement.

This question of mothers on the fast track is of great interest to me as someone who is part of a generation that saw major shifts in workplace opportunities for women. I myself was able to walk through newly opened doors and balanced my own juggling act. My graduate students, 4,000 of them over the years, have shown me that women's experiences have not been dramatically simplified in recent years. I've watched many capable women struggle to find their own way. The question is even more pressing for the generation of my daughter and co-author, Eve Mason Ekman. As a twenty-six-year-old graduate from a master's program, Eve is part of a group of young women now passing into adulthood without clear models for how to have a career and family but facing a path strewn with obstacles. "When is a good time to have a baby" may not be a question that every twenty-six-year-old thinks to ask herself. But few young women even consider that the fertility window is at odds with career ambitions, which means that finding new pathways and solutions—and soon—for this new generation of mothers is invested with utmost importance.

In my first year as graduate dean, I formed a research team to study how family formation affects the careers of both men and women in academia over the course of their lives. We called our pursuit the Do Babies Matter? project. The name stuck because it points to the heart of the matter, often skirted by those who believe there is equal opportunity in America today. It also touches a nerve for young women entering the fast track who wonder what family compromises they will have to make in order to succeed.

After making some surprising discoveries in academic fields, we decided to expand our investigation to include other fast track careers in law, science, medicine, and the corporate world.[6] We believed that finding similar patterns in these career tracks would indicate that we were discovering the shape and challenge of motherhood in all fast track professions.

My daughter requested that we add the media world, her chosen career field. Journalism in all forms—newspaper and magazines, TV, and radio broadcasting—attracts talented, ambitious women. Although the career track for women in these professions does not require a graduate degree as an entry-level requirement, the similarities are still more compelling than the differences. The long-term career track in media looks much like the other fast track professions, with a disproportionate density of women in the lower ranks and

Married with Children

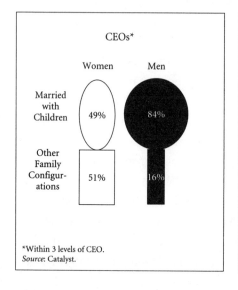

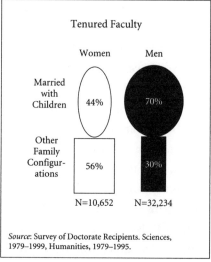

only a scattered few at the top. These women are far less likely to be married with children.

All of these male-dominated professions now have a significant representation of women, and all have begun to investigate the career paths of female employees over time. Each offers adequate or better data sources for study. The best of these data sets is the Survey of Doctorate Recipients (sponsored largely by the National Science Foundation), which tracks 160,000 Ph.D.'s in all disciplines throughout their career until age seventy-six. The American Bar Association and the American Medical Association have also undertaken long-term surveys of the career lives of men and women. *Catalyst*, a business journal, and a variety of other professional organizations have surveyed men and women in the corporate world. The 2000 U.S. census also offers a rich snapshot of Americans' experience with family and career.

Our investigation uncovered stunning similarities across these professions and revealed the common problems experienced by fast track professionals. Initially our careful study of numbers and trends didn't explain exactly why some women drop out and why others stay the course and reach the top. We had framed the problems but not the solutions. Finally we realized that an effective way to complement the research was to learn from the experiences of individual women struggling and succeeding with these very issues. One of the core components of this book is based on identifying and interviewing women in fast track professions. Almost all of these interviews were conducted by my daughter, Eve Ekman.

The issues raised in this book aren't just an academic matter for me. Coming of professional age during the women's movement in the late 1960s, I rode the ups and downs of history through the last third of the twentieth century. I was part of the first large wave of women to enter a doctoral program; in my case American history, which is still my passion. When I entered graduate school, an unusual choice for a woman, I considered this accomplishment to be entirely my own. I was unaware that my generous fellowship and very welcoming graduate program were products of the galloping economy of the times, which created a huge growth in higher education and opportunities for Ph.D.'s to fill the faculty ranks of burgeoning new state universities.

I was also an unknowing beneficiary of the civil rights movement that had begun in the 1950s and later the new feminist movement. In 1966 author-activist Betty Friedan put down her pen to take to the streets after her surprise best-seller *The Feminine Mystique,* which sharply critiqued 1950s domesticity.

Friedan and fifteen other professional women founded what became the National Organization for Women (NOW) in a hotel room in 1966. Friedan and Dr. Pauli Murray coauthored NOW's original statement of purpose, which began, "The purpose of NOW is to take action to bring women into full participation in the mainstream of American society now, exercising all the privileges and responsibilities thereof in truly equal partnership with men."

What brought these women together was gender inequality in the workplace and lax enforcement of employment discrimination laws that had been extended to include gender. Most male-dominated professions like law, medicine, and the corporate world were closed to them. Breaching these enclaves of power was breaking through the "glass ceiling." In addition, true gender equality, they decided, had to occur both in the workplace and in the home; men and women must share equally in all aspects of domestic life, including child rearing.[7]

But the strongly individualistic rhetoric of the feminist movement didn't always match women's personal experiences or desires. From the beginning of my graduate studies, I was torn between family and career. Like many of my classmates, I had married one month after graduating from college in 1965. And like most women of that era (and many today), I deferred to my husband's career. His job brought us to California, where the job market for women with newly minted Ph.D.'s was still closed. My only options were poorly paid part-time lecturer positions, which I pursued while completing my degree. Our son, Tom, was born in 1972, and after a lot of agonizing, I chose to pursue law—a profession I believed would offer more opportunities and fewer geographical constraints.

I did not do well in the probationary period of law practice, also known as the associate years. My husband and I divorced and I gave up law after a year, unable to deal with the demands of work and home. With few friends or relatives to help with child care, I could not manage the long hours required to succeed as an associate. Although I considered myself a failure for leaving the practice of law, I have come to understand that women often consider such choices personal failures, even when there are no real options. Even mothers with a stable marriage and a strong support system struggle to hold on to their career during these difficult make-or-break years.

For nearly a decade I worked in the "second tier" as a midlevel, non–tenure track academic administrator at a small college. These years gave me breathing space to focus on my family obligations, remarry, and welcome my second child, Eve, in 1980.

Unlike thousands of other women who have stepped or fallen into the second tier to accommodate family obligations, I was given a second chance when my children were older. I was offered an entry-level, tenure-track faculty position at UC Berkeley at age forty-four. For someone over forty to be hired for an entry-level position in any of the fast track professions is unusual. The "résumé gap"—the years between the completion of training and the first fast track job—usually damns the applicant's résumé to the "no interview" pile. In fact the central administration initially turned down my appointment because of my age, but a strong dean championed my cause.

I was offered this opportunity because I wrote a book in the late 1980s while working in the second tier. This accomplishment was made possible by a six-month break to accompany my husband on his sabbatical to England. That precious time, with our children in English schools, allowed me to rethink, retool, and begin a book. Having struggled—and failed—to make it on the fast track, I had personal insight for my book, *The Equality Trap (1988)*, which expressed concern about encouraging women to run on the fast track without changing the track itself to accommodate families. I marshaled my historical and legal knowledge to make the best case I could for transforming the workplace. In retrospect, I suspect I was also trying to make sense of my own failure.

The rare opportunity to return to academia after years in the second tier was a defining point in my career. I was able to deal with the stressful make-or-break years leading to tenure in large part because I was older and more experienced, and my children were older. Eve, then nine, and Tom, sixteen, no longer made the exceptional time demands of early childhood. They were healthy and engaged in their school and social communities. And my husband Paul Ekman, also a professor, was a helpmate both emotionally and financially.

My years as a professor, and more recently as graduate dean, have been deeply satisfying, just as I had hoped they would be years ago as a graduate student. Although my story is exceptional in some ways, it reflects the critical work–family junctures that often halt or sidetrack women's professional trajectories.

Our goal in this book is to help finish the task that my generation began when we opened professional doors for women to assume an equal place alongside men in the workplace and at home. This book offers a road map of how careers unfold, what to expect at each stage of life, and how to maneuver each obstacle in order to achieve life goals.

For women like my graduate students, who work hard to contribute to their chosen profession and have a family, I hope the material and advice in these pages will make the road ahead more manageable. This book is also for men like my male graduate students. Transformative structural changes in the workplace to accommodate family must work for them as well, or they will fail. They must have the opportunity to become full participants in raising their children. Finally this book is for Eve's generation, to help young professional women in all professions understand their struggle and inform the choices that they make in order to create the new paradigms for family and career success.

—Mary Ann Mason

While many women of my generation experience anxiety over the sheer number of career choices facing us, we often forget that just three decades ago the opportunity to pursue a career in any arena was not a given. In one respect the women of my mother's generation had it easier: there were clear directions for how they should proceed after graduation. For my mother and her friends, receiving a wedding band soon after accepting a college diploma was the norm and husbands' careers came first. But current graduates will find no prescribed path once they receive their degree. Young professionals focus their time on developing and pursuing their individual identity and career. Our generation treasures a prolonged single period that lasts well through the twenties and often into the thirties. Young women and men focus on their careers before considering their future family plans. The interviews I conducted for this book have given me the opportunity to consider the paths chosen by the women navigating this freedom and family bind.

None of the successful mothers I interviewed consider themselves superwomen. They believe that most mothers can do what they have done, and they freely share their strategies. Several common strategies cross generations and professions: time management skills, knowing when to say no, and controlling "mother guilt." Almost all of these women experienced remorse (mother guilt) at some point and worried that they were not spending enough time with their children, but they all found ways to manage their anxiety and pursue their career goals.

These successful women offered thoughtful suggestions about structural reforms that are or should be in place, which would make their professions more family friendly and the second tier a better option. Many of these structural changes focus on the make-or-break years, roughly the decade between ages thirty and forty—the period of maximum demand that occurs at the beginning of the fast track career and leads to tenure, partnership, or CEO. During these years the time demands of work make parenthood nearly impossible for women, yet these are the years that offer women their last chance at parenthood. The career clock and the biological clock are on a collision course. It is during the make-or-break years that most women drop out of the fast track.

Yet women make the decisions that determine their career paths during the student and young adult years, often based on little information and few role models. And again later in life, those who survive the make-or-break years must still deal with obstacles to leadership, which often prevent them from shattering the second glass ceiling and achieving the highest positions in their profession. I interviewed these pioneer women in their bay view offices, in former gentlemen's clubs, and in their homes—from a minimansion in Oakland to an elegant apartment overlooking Central Park. These women, now poised and powerful, had been on the front lines, battling their way into positions that were not considered theirs to occupy. Some were met with overt bias and even ridicule, and most faced undercutting and invisibility. Yet they prevailed. These are their stories.

—Eve Mason Ekman

Mothers on
   the Fast Track

1

The "Mother Problem": Up, Out, or Sidelined?

Recently I gave a talk on career and motherhood to an audience at a medical school. Several young mothers with babies attended, as they usually do at such talks. One young woman named Kara, carrying an infant on her chest in a Snugli, approached me after the talk and proudly related that she had her daughter during her third year of residency. "It was rough but my team all pitched in. I was home for six weeks. When I came back I arranged to have my baby-sitter come to the hospital for nursing," she said, beaming at her daughter.

Later that afternoon at the reception, I was speaking with a senior faculty member and mentioned Kara and the other young women with babies. "Yes, these young mothers are remarkable," he said. "They'll make good doctors, but they won't make good scientists." I asked him what he meant. He hesitated. "It's not that they're not smart—they're really top-notch—but they don't have the stamina for the long run—you know, the grants, tenure, and all that. They make their choices; we all make our choices." Clearly in the eyes of this faculty member, a contemporary of mine, even women who can successfully navigate the obstacles of the medical profession are not able to meet the strenuous demands of the basic science research field.

Almost every week the media pick up another story about women with expensive professional degrees "opting out" of corporate executive positions or partnerships in major law firms to have children. These so-called elite women often express relief after escaping the competitive rat race and describe a new joy at discovering the wonders of motherhood. Yet these same media outlets also announce the elevation of yet another woman to the presidency of an Ivy League college, casually discuss women as possible presidential candidates, and laud the promotion of another woman as a TV news anchor.

These mixed messages portray an inconsistent picture that can make it difficult to decipher what is really going on. Are women slowly but relentlessly

rising to equal representation in top positions so routinely that the phenomenon no longer requires media fanfare? Or are these women dropping
out at a faster rate than they can succeed?

The short answer is, Most women aren't doing either—they are not steadily
rising to equal representation in top positions, nor are they dropping out in
large numbers. Our research shows that highly educated women rarely leave
their chosen profession entirely. Instead they become caught in a "second tier"
within or allied with their profession where they take breaks for family needs
but return to work, sometimes on a reduced schedule but frequently full-time,
until retirement.

These women enter prestigious career tracks after many years of education
and apprenticeship and then encounter a workplace where sacrifices of family
life become more daunting and models for success more scarce. They enter
a second tier, unlikely to regain their position on the fast track. For many
women the second tier has become the default "mommy track." It covers a
wide range of jobs, from well-compensated positions with reduced hours in
health maintenance organizations (HMOs) or biotech firms to part-time
lecturer positions with no security or benefits. There are many virtues of a less
time-consuming alternative, but in the current workplace, many of these jobs
are insecure, underpaid, undervalued. What second tier jobs have in common
is that mothers are overrepresented and there is no track to the top.

The medical resident mom whom I met after my lecture is statistically
headed for the second tier. Although we did not discuss her long-range career
plans, she told me her residency is in pediatrics, one of the primary care specialties where young women, now about half of medical school classes, gravi-
tate in great numbers.[1] She is likely to join an HMO or large group practice
where she can gain control of her hours. She may reduce her weekly contribution to four days a week and limit her on-call time. She will earn com-
pensated positions with reduced hours in health maintenance organizations
at pay significantly less than male physicians'.[2]

It is possible, though statistically unlikely, that she is planning a career in
academic medicine. Only about 15 percent of full professors in medical schools
are women, and there are just nine women medical school deans in the United
States.[3] This route is long and arduous. After residency, a specialized fellowship in, say, pediatric oncology, a first grant, and one or two publications will
prepare her for an entry-level assistant professor position. More grants and
continuing publications will pave the route to the relative security of tenure.

It is not difficult to understand why few women who choose to have a family pursue academic medicine. The question is, Do they have a choice? The competitive world of medical science waits for no one. A year or two out of the competitive grant race and there is no longer a place at the table. The first woman president of Princeton, Shirley Tilghman, who was appointed in 2004, famously argued that the tenure system should be dropped because it's "'no friend to women'." It makes huge demands at a time when women are already stressed out with young families.[4]

Consequently the second tier represents a viable alternative, usually the only one. For many it is an opportunity to stay in a profession while having children and hoping for a second chance down the road. Other workers, both men and women, are not interested in the frantic pace that usually characterizes rising to the top of the profession. They find the slower pace and lower expectations of the second tier more congenial. Indeed, for some, the second tier provides a welcome respite from rigid professions that offered few schedule choices beyond the full-time track. For example, Internet entrepreneur Tiffany Shlain's second tier schedule allows her to take time for her family throughout her workday: "I get time to run errands, take my daughter to the doctor, have time with the girls," she enthuses.

But again, the key is for women to have choices; mothers should have the option to try out a part-time schedule like Tiffany's when children are young or the opportunity to stay at a Fortune 500 company and the right to return to a full-time position after family obligations ease up.

As this book will show, women do not choose the second tier in one decisive moment. When we read stories on the brilliant careers of successful women or careers eagerly left behind to pursue full-time motherhood, we see only a snapshot in time. Yet a series of decisions are made consciously or unconsciously over the span of a career—from the day a student enters college to the day she retires.

Kara, the medical resident, probably began her medical studies majoring in biology, the science that has been most welcoming to women; the percentage of degrees awarded to women has soared from 25 percent to 50 percent.[5] A biology degree positions women to enter medical school, where their numbers have swelled to 45 percent of entering classes.[6] Medical students are only part of the incredible wave of women pouring into professional schools, which are now comprised of roughly even numbers of women and men.[7]

When women are choosing career directions, the question of marriage and babies is largely abstract. The age at which women college graduates have their first baby has risen dramatically. In 1970, 73 percent of college-educated women had their first baby by thirty, while in 2000, only 36 percent did so in that time frame.[8] This incredible shift in large part reflects greater opportunities—and a greater necessity—for women to participate in the workforce. Women planning careers that require advanced training further postpone the idea of family; they are not likely to have children, if they do at all, until well into their thirties.[9] Students like Kara who attend graduate and professional programs are delaying decisions in other ways. Both men and women are likely to take off a year or two after college and delay their advanced training until they are twenty-five or older.

Settled into their graduate and professional training, men and women appear on equal footing. With notable exceptions in engineering and the physical sciences, women are well represented in all fields and almost no one—male or female—has children. This even balance begins to change as students approach age thirty. But ironically, men students, with their nearly limitless biological clock, begin to marry and have children before women do.[10] Women students delay child bearing in large part because they are afraid of not being taken seriously in their educational and career pursuits. For men, however, fatherhood is considered a mark of maturity.

Approaching thirty, many women reevaluate their long-term career plans. Medical students, like Kara, look hard at the future. Earlier plans for a surgical specialty or a research career in oncology may be jettisoned in light of the years that these specialties require—six to ten in surgery and a similar number in research oncology. Pediatrics, in contrast, requires just three to four years of additional training. And all residencies are notoriously demanding, with eighty-hour weeks the norm. It is difficult to plan a family in this time frame. In other fields a shift in focus may mean repositioning toward employment in industry rather than continuing a postdoc in research or deciding on a small firm rather than the highly competitive race of a large firm.

It is between ages thirty and forty that women change career direction. This is the decade, which I call the "make-or-break" years, when women are mostly likely to drop into the second tier. The demands of a first job in the fast track male-dominated professions are daunting. This is the time when sixty- to eighty-hour work weeks are not uncommon and when extreme flexibility, including moving or constant travel, is often a job requirement.

But for women, this probationary period also coincides with the decisive years for motherhood. Very few women have children after age forty. Among aspiring physicians like Kara, one-half will have their first child during their residency when they are likely to be in their thirties.[11] Mothers, but not fathers, will take some time out of the workplace, from a few months to a few years. They may hope to return to the fast track position they left, but most will fall into a second tier position.

Some mothers persevere on the fastest track and do not take extended leave. They excel at work while putting in a second shift—the norm for all working mothers—at home. And they each deal with the unique obstacles of their professions. Recently I received an e-mail from a mother with young children under four who had followed the difficult route to academic medicine. After successfully navigating residencies and research fellowships, she is currently an assistant professor in neurology at a major medical school. But she has a new challenge to face: the federal government. Like most medical researchers, she relies completely on federal grants to pursue her research and pay her salary. In the competitive world of scientific grants, presentations at conferences are necessary to stay in the game. But there is little room for family accommodation in the federal grant world. She wrote, "I called NIH to ask whether my grant could help me pay the baby-sitter who will allow me to go to the meeting and present data from the project, and the program officer (a woman) basically laughed in my face. Do you think it was an unreasonable question?"

The uncompromising, competitive nature of science takes its toll and some women research scientists consider giving up, even after they have achieved a degree of success. But this is only part of the answer. What explains the exodus of women from the fast track across all the professions? Is it the famously unreformed structure of the family? Fathers now spend demonstrably more hours with their children, but mothers still put in the same "second shift." Or is it the social culture, which seems to place renewed moral restraints on mothers to focus their full attention on child raising to the exclusion of their own interests or concerns? Or perhaps it is the shadowy "old boy's network," which persists in a tamed state after decades of sexual discrimination and sexual harassment lawsuits.

The explanation in fact encompasses all of the above, applied with different intensity and professional variations over the occupational life of high-achieving women.

At age forty those still on the fast track look a lot different than they did at thirty, when they completed their training. Attrition during the make-or-break years has culled the herd of young professional women. Many of those who remain will be married but, depending on the profession, only 40 to 60 percent will have children.[12] The survivors of the make-or-break years are now mostly married men with children.

Mothers who endure the make-or-break years do well in their professions. They pass through the first glass ceiling to senior positions, but few make it to the very top—the positions of greatest power and influence, those above the "second glass ceiling." The percentage of women at the very top has grown in recent years, but it is by no means proportional to the numbers who have poured into the professional fields. This is not just a time lag; women continue to be stuck in the second tier, and mothers who persist often lose momentum.

All of these factors contribute to a distinct trend: rather than achieving equal representation at the top where decisions are made and new discoveries brought forth, women are stalled in the lower tier of increasingly bifurcated occupations. They will have less say in decisions made for and about them. A woman's voice at the top can make a difference. It can offer new perspectives and new ideas regarding the structure of the workplace.

With few women on medical school faculties, the future course of medical training will be taught, as it always has been, from a male perspective. With few women faculty or scientists to inspire new students, women will no longer believe that all possibilities are open to them, and soon they will not be. Women will not be chosen for training in academic medicine or surgical specialties because they will not be considered serious players. They will be treated as they were fifty years ago when male-dominated professions held that women weren't worth the gamble.

The powerful institutions of law, medicine, the university world, and business steer the course of the nation. Women have poured into these workplaces in the past thirty years because they must and because they can. But without a strong voice at the top, women will continue to be second-class workers and their point of view will not be considered in the critical issues of the day—whether octogenarians receive medical benefits, if or when to re-strict interrogation or abortion, the appropriate wage to pay a piece worker in Mexico, or how to handle compensation and retirement plans for employees.

There is another loss. These highly trained women will not have the opportunity to experience the challenges and satisfactions for which they have spent years preparing. They will never attain their full potential; the level of status, security, and income that they are qualified to receive. Observing the dearth of women partners, fewer than 20 percent nationally, the president of the Los Angeles County Bar Association observed, "We have a long way to go. It's my dream that more women will stick it out in the law until they get to the fun part and it just breaks my heart to see them giving up."[13]

SOLVING THE "MOTHER PROBLEM"

The key to advancement is figuring out the "mother problem." We can all agree that children are a wonder and a blessing, not a problem; but motherhood is. Child rearing does not occur in a vacuum; decisions about motherhood are bound up with societal expectations, the nature of the workplace (and how it works for or against mothers), and women's personal needs during the various life stages. Solutions must address all of these factors if they are to succeed.

There is reason for hope. There are more women in top leadership positions than ever before, and others are coming through the ranks. The numbers are far smaller than what they should be, but far greater than they were thirty years ago. And there is a growing national awareness that retaining highly trained professionals will necessitate making serious changes to the structure of the workplace. Closer to home, universities, arguably the most conservative of American institutions, are beginning to change. In the past few years, unprecedented reforms to the tenure system, including extended parental leave policies and part-time options with right of full return, have occurred. These changes were made because our studies and others made it clear that we would lose our competitive edge with each other and in the global competition for the best talent if we did not do so. The business world is increasingly aware of the cost of losing its best-trained professionals. A recent study of eighty-seven leading companies reported in the *Wall Street Journal* showed that 59 percent now offered "extended" paid maternity leave pay—beyond the normal six to eight weeks disability pay offered at most companies. Other firms are "sweetening the pot" by offering positions without travel to new mothers to lure them back to the workplace. One company found that it retained 86 percent of its new mothers, compared to 63 percent before the innovative new policies were in place.[14]

This chapter frames the themes of motherhood over the career span. As an overview, however, it does not describe the differences between professions—the unique obstacles and the special advantages of each; why, for instance, women doctors are the most satisfied and the least likely to leave their profession, or why women scientists are rarely elected to the National Academy of Sciences. It also does not explain why many mothers succeed in spite of professional obstacles while others drop into the second tier or abandon their career entirely. The following chapters will closely examine the lives of women in different professions as they work their way through their student years, their critical make-or-break years and beyond into the leadership years. The problem areas are targeted, but so are the solutions. In the words of Jessica, a lawyer mother we will meet in a later chapter, "I love my family and I love my work. I have only one life to lead and I want it to be the best it can be, that means a balanced life; and believe me, I am not a superwoman."

The pendulum could swing either way—the doors to the top professions were opened to women amid huge fanfare in the 1970s and 1980s with federal legislation, sex discrimination lawsuits, and organized collective action. But these advances have been tempered by women's limited professional upward mobility. Without further advance, women may become permanently marginalized in the second tier as the doors to the room at the top close again.

Such changes are essential at this critical point in the history of women and work. Women have always worked. They have worked on the farm, in the factories, and at home. My immigrant grandmother rarely left her Minnesota home except for trips to the grocery store and church, but it served as a boardinghouse for five iron ore miners in addition to her family of five for whom she cooked and cleaned. Now more than ever before in American history, women, including most mothers, are working outside the home. It's the challenge of the next generation to ensure that woman have equal opportunities in all careers in the future, including those in the elite professional and managerial classes.

2

The Student Years:
Eighteen to Thirty-Two

Of the female students in my starting class [of biology Ph.D. students], none of my colleagues became faculty and two dropped out. Most of them have to make a decision when they hit their late twenties or early thirties. They either have to quit or take a breather.
—Jennifer Mitchell, neuroscience postdoc

Choosing to enter a high-status male-dominated profession requires years of additional training, financial sacrifice, and hard work. Students who aspire to become doctors, for example, must have the drive, talent, and focus to survive and thrive in cutthroat premed programs in order to get into medical school. If they do make it past this stage, they will likely spend the next six to ten years in equally demanding training as medical students and later as residents. They will be paid a pittance or nothing at all during this period, and, like their counterparts in law and MBA programs, they will likely accumulate significant debt. Some of these ambitious young women—especially those in science—may encounter discrimination and an uncompromising, female- and family-unfriendly environment.

Talented young women make these sacrifices because they are inspired by their chosen field, they wish to contribute, and they believe they will be successful professionals once they've completed this arduous preparation period. Indeed, women are entering graduate programs in record numbers with the confidence that they will be successful in their careers. And many are.

Yet it wasn't so long ago that the U.S. court system upheld the belief that a woman's place is in the home. In 1873 the Supreme Court ruled in *Bradwell v. Illinois* that the Fourteenth Amendment's equal protection clause did not guarantee women the right to practice law. "The harmony, not to say identity, of interests and views which belong, or should belong, to the family institution is repugnant to the ideas of a woman adopting a distinct and independent career from that of her husband."

Today this opinion seems arcane, even laughable. Gender parity in higher and professional education has been one of the remarkable accomplishments of the last third of the twentieth century, and now seems commonplace. In fact, women have overtaken men among new college freshman—in 2000, 57.2 percent of undergraduate college degrees were awarded to women.[1] About half of law school and medical school graduates are now women, as are half of all Ph.D. recipients.

Women as a Percentage of Professional and Doctoral Recipients in the U.S., 1966–2000

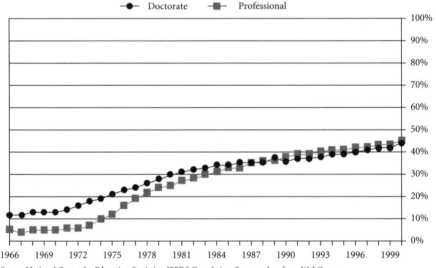

Source: National Center for Education Statistics, *IPEDS Completions Survey,* taken from WebCaspar (IPEDS includes doctorate records file data).

Contemporary college women have more career options because of the doors opened by civil rights legislation; Title VII, which forbids gender discrimination in the workplace; Title IX, which insists on gender equity in education; and the women's movement, which fought to enforce these new laws. For thirty years, the idea of equality in education and the workplace has so completely permeated everyday rhetoric that young women almost believe they no longer face gender discrimination.

Women of my generation faced a very different scenario. For the pioneers, the first generation to push into male-dominated professions in the 1970s, the student years were colored by the prospect of family, and academic and career opportunities were not a given.

My own career choices were framed by early marriage and the closed doors of most male professions. In the 1960s, I was a twenty-year-old junior at Vassar—then a women-only college. At the time, most education on the East Coast was segregated by sex. The Ivy League colleges were all male with a few sister colleges attached, and state universities elsewhere around the county, while coed, were largely dominated by male student bodies. At Vassar the education was serious and rigorous, but the career choices recommended for women were different from those promoted for men at men's colleges or for men at coed universities.

In the 1960s, only 10 percent of Ph.D. degrees nationally were earned by women, and a large portion of those were in education.[2] Married women rarely took this route; it was mostly brainy single women who boldly chose scholarly careers (and their mothers worried that they'd never "catch" a man because of it). Women were even less likely to enter law school or medicine; only 7 percent of medical degrees and 8 percent of law degrees were granted to women in 1966.[3]

My women professors had been raised in an earlier wave of American feminism, the suffragettes of the early twentieth century. They had come of age in an era when women pursued the vote, often taking to the streets to assert their demands. Many of these activist women chose male professions and did not have children. They did not agonize over career versus marriage or over marriage in addition to career. They saw it as an either/or decision. Only 50 percent of those graduating from women's colleges like Vassar in 1890 married, and most of the unmarried pursued a career. By 1900 women were represented in virtually all the male-dominated professions. Women with great courage and tough skins had demanded and won places in medicine, law, journalism, and higher education. The proportion of women in medicine, 7 percent, persisted until the 1970s.[4]

In my pioneer generation, women were expected to marry early, marry well, and follow their husband's career. Men were expected to be the sole breadwinners; pursuing a professional career was a man's route to economic security. Like my female classmates, I believed that if I worked at all, it would be at a "job" and not a career, perhaps teaching for a few years before having children. During my senior year, my friends proudly flashed new engagement rings every week. My own wedding was planned for July following graduation and my plans were clear: my husband would complete a Ph.D. in science and I would teach history at a high school wherever he secured a position as a scientist. Fortunately my life took a different course, thanks to a mentor who helped me think beyond these limited horizons. Such guidance, as we shall see, is a key determinant of women's success during the formative student years when women are faced for the first time with critical career and family choices.

THE DOOR NOT OPENED: THE PHYSICAL SCIENCES

In spite of important strides we have made in bringing gender equality to graduate and professional education, there are still pockets of gender discrimination, particularly in engineering, math, and the physical sciences, where the number of women, although improved, is still consistently low.

In 2005 the president of Harvard University, Lawrence Summers, speaking at an academic conference on women and underrepresented minorities in science, raised the question of whether innate gender differences affecting ability might help explain why fewer women succeed in science and engineering careers. Summer's remarks, delivered to a small group of professors, were soon heard around the world.

Why does the stereotype that women are not bright enough for mathematical hard thinking persist? A substantial body of research has shown that socialization from an early age, rather than aptitude, is the major reason that women leave the sciences. Not only are women regarded as mothers or potential mothers who won't put their careers first, they are also seen by many as not quite good enough in the first place.

These attitudes may help explain why the physical sciences and engineering remain stubbornly male-dominated enclaves with only small cells of women. Women receive less than a quarter of the doctorates awarded to American students in the physical sciences, including computer science and math, and only about 15 percent of the engineering doctorates.[5] The numbers are improving but are too low to allow us to confidently predict equity at any time in the future.

Elga Wasserman, author of *The Door in the Dream: Conversations with Eminent Women in Science*, notes that many of the obstacles that contemporary women scientists encounter are rooted in a disconnect between the realities of women's lives and assumptions about their lives based on traditional stereotypes that remain entrenched in our society.[6]

At the core of this stereotype is motherhood. Some scientists may believe that women who have families cannot be serious scientists because academic science demands exclusive attention to research. Ironically, research shows that male scientists are far more likely to have children than women scientists; two years after their Ph.D.'s, nearly 50 percent of men, but only 30 percent of women, had children.[7]

Dr. Robert C. Nicholson, Nobel Prize winner in physics and chair of the National Science Board panel that investigated why the brightest American students aren't pursuing advanced science degrees, believes part of the problem is the lab culture that requires punishingly long hours in a hierarchical structure. He concludes, "To get more women, we probably need to restructure work environments in labs and universities so that they're more responsive to them in their childbearing years."[8]

MARRIAGE AND THE "TWO BODY PROBLEM"

While graduate school is a time to refine academic and professional skills, it's also a time when many women consider marriage and family. By the time they are in their early thirties, about 54 percent of male Ph.D.'s and 49 percent of female Ph.D.'s are married.[9]

Contemporary women hold few expectations of early marriage and childbirth. Indeed for women like my daughter Eve, now twenty-six, the prospect of marriage and motherhood remains distant and abstract. In 1960 the average bride was 20.3 years old—meaning that nearly half of all brides were still in their teens—and grooms averaged 23 years. By 2000, the median age had risen to 25.1 for brides, 26.8 for grooms, and even later for college graduates. Overall, more education means later marriage and children.[10]

Women are more likely than men to marry a fellow student, and during this time bargains are struck about which careers are chosen, where to locate following graduation, whose career takes precedence, and who will earn more money.

For me, there was no bargaining process. My husband was three years older, he finished his Ph.D. first, and he received a job offer for a postdoctoral fellowship at Berkeley. Even if he had not been ahead of me, I would have deferred to his career, which was the accepted practice for women at the time. I did not face a rosy career future; in the whole University of California nine-campus system, only 1.3 women (one part-time) held faculty positions in history. The reality of marriage, and soon a child, stopped me from considering a move to the East Coast or anywhere else. My choices were part-time positions, a course here and there, and the life of a gypsy scholar.

Today's young student couples often approach this two-career bind in a more egalitarian way. They cling to the ideal of equality and may agree to take turns when it comes time to move for careers—his choice for now, hers later. They may even decide to take jobs in different cities, which is an increasingly common choice for academic couples where jobs are limited and specialized. The future prospect of children can play an important part in this bargaining process. But our research shows that ultimately women are more likely to defer to men.[11]

We call it the "two body problem" in the university world, where jobs are extremely specialized; even in a metropolitan area like San Francisco, there are few universities to choose from. Universities or research institutes can rarely accommodate both bodies. One body must defer, and that body is likely to be hers. Young mothers will also defer to the perceived needs of their children or the need for stability.

Karie Frasch met her partner Barb, then a medical student, when she was a graduate student at Berkeley. Karie wanted to have a child but not during graduate school, believing she wouldn't finish her social science Ph.D. degree if she did so. "My vision of my life always included kids *and* career. As I got farther along, I started thinking about what I was going to do next. I didn't have much flexibility because Barb's life was already set. I couldn't just take a job anywhere in the country because Barb was already in med school here."

Karie received her degree, had a baby, and took a half-time research job at a university instead of a faculty position. She remains undecided about her future career plans.

Careers in law, medicine, and the corporate world may offer more options in a metropolitan area, but still the pull of the better job, the best route to the top, will force choices between couples and cause some women to exit the fast track even during the student years.

STUDENT PARENTS

The great majority of college-educated women, 64 percent, will not have their first baby, if they have children at all, before age thirty.[12] Young women today believe they should have years to focus on their own development and careers without the hindrance of family obligations. Not many babies are born during the student years. Exact figures are elusive, but overall only about 10 percent of graduate and professional students at Berkeley are parents at the time of graduation—and these are more likely to be men than women.[13] The great exception to this rule is medical residencies (which will receive special attention in the next chapter); about half of first babies are born during these grueling years.[14]

Why do most women defer having a child during their student years? After all, it's a period when they have more flexible schedules and the possibility of a community with which to share the experience of parenting. Students defer this decision for the same reasons that I did thirty years ago—they fear that they will not be taken seriously and that their professors, mentors, and future employees will discourage them from continuing.

Rena Scott, a Berkeley law student, does not intend to have children anytime soon. For a law firm, losing a trained lawyer to maternity leave or a part-time track, she believes, is a serious liability. "Mommy lawyers are usually not partners, but daddy lawyers are." She claims this disconnect is almost accepted wisdom among her classmates. "I have to think about how it will affect my career. Now when I hear the word 'kids,' I think 'death to my career,' and that's sad."

Women in Ph.D. programs, particularly in the sciences and engineering, perceive a "no children allowed" rule in the prevailing climate. Childbirth may delay the completion of degree and stand in the way of important professional opportunities, summer internships, and appearances at professional conferences. Most importantly the professors and mentors who are in a position to advance women's careers may pass them over for special recommendation if they believe they'll be less likely to succeed. Marriage and pregnancy negatively impact women's careers in academic science at three critical junctures: pregnancy during graduate school, marriage at the point of seeking a job, and pregnancy prior to tenure.

These often anguished decisions have profound implications for their future earning power, career success, and family structure. Often there is no real choice.

"I don't think I'll ever be able to do a tenure track job and people were very upfront with me about that when I had my child," recounts Jennifer Mitchell, who had her first child soon after completing her Ph.D. "Looking around me, I see that people are completely shut out of positions because of family."

For some, the fear that motherhood will derail their careers is realized. Postdoctoral fellow Sherry Towers, a particle physicist, was effectively blacklisted by her adviser when she had a baby. When she was pregnant he said he would refuse to write a letter of recommendation for her unless she returned almost immediately. Even though she did return quickly, he still refused and she received no interviews for any of the positions she applied for.[15] Postdocs are particularly vulnerable, since their careers depend completely on the faculty supervisor who accepts them in his or her laboratory.

Our own study of postdoctoral students at Berkeley reveals the conflicts and discouragement experienced by many postdocs who are mothers. Postdoctoral fellowships are now a routine extension of professional training past the Ph.D. level for students in the biological sciences and, increasingly, in other sciences and social sciences. Because the students are somewhat older, usually in their early thirties, postdocs are more likely to be married and to have children.[16] We asked both men and women postdocs whether they were

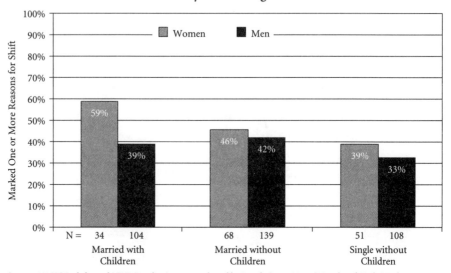

**Postdocs Who Say
They Are Leaving Science**

Source: 1999 UC Berkeley and LBNL Postdoc Survey, conducted by Joseph Cerny, Maresi Nerad, and Linda McPheron.

considering changing careers away from academic research. Fifty-nine percent of the women with children said they were. Not surprisingly, they indicated that their greatest concern was balancing career and family.[17]

These women believed they had already lost the race. They spoke of their decision to leave their career track as a choice, but in the fast-paced world of science, the choice was not entirely their own.[18] Married postdoc men with children still managed to work about as many hours in the lab and attend as many conferences as other men. Presumably they did not work a full second shift at home.[19]

THE FIRST CUT

As they approach the three decade mark toward the end of their training, most women, partnered or not, consider the question of career choice in light of present or future family obligations. It may not be the first time they have thought of this issue, but now the matter is of some urgency. They know their biological clock has limits. They must make choices that will determine their life's work, and they must evaluate how and when having children will fit into

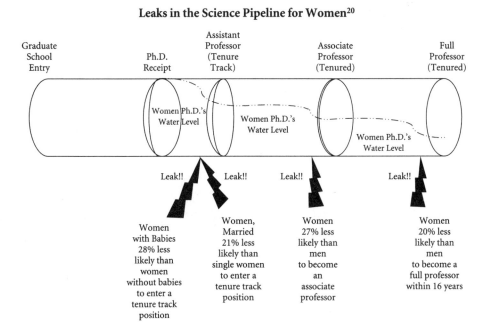

Leaks in the Science Pipeline for Women[20]

this choice—if at all. As previously noted, many women at this point do not stick to their original career goals. They may work part-time, change direction, or simply take a break.

As they look forward, the demanding requirements of fast track professions set in. When Karie Frasch finished her Ph.D. at Berkeley and began considering motherhood, her career track suddenly looked less appealing. "I went into graduate school thinking a faculty position would be a great way to have kids, that there is flexibility and open summers. Then as I began to see professors who had kids totally strung out and stressed out I began to realize, wait, I am not going to do that!"

In science and engineering, women's early departure from a university research career is dramatic, and is nearly always driven by family concerns. Strikingly, our research shows single women are as likely as men to secure a job at a major research institution; they remain on the fast track.[21]

SUPPORT SYSTEMS: MENTORS, MOTHERS, AND ROLE MODELS

Women students, especially those in the hard sciences, have historically faced and continue to confront obstacles to fast track success. And yet most will graduate. These hearty graduates are talented, driven, and ambitious. Also, they are likely to have benefited from the support of mentors, advisers, and role models who champion their cause and offer guidance and encouragement. This is as true for this generation as it was for the pioneer generation. Sometimes that role model is their original female prototype—their mother. Other times it's a key academic adviser who suggests future career directions, guides student research, and serves as a role model. In the sciences, the role of a high-profile mentor is crucial. The most distinguished professors work on the hottest topics—areas that are expected to break significant new ground rather than refine current knowledge. When a topic is hot, several groups of scientists often compete to solve it, and enormous prestige is attached to getting there first.[22]

Advisers can help or hurt students' careers, and women can be at a disadvantage if they get stuck with a faculty mentor with deep-seated gender biases. Lola Odessya related to me that after she had received her Ph.D. in chemical engineering from Berkeley in four years (nearly record speed for a

Ph.D.), her adviser not only failed to help her secure her first job but didn't even ask about her plans. I came to know Lola as the effective, articulate president of the Graduate Student Assembly, the representative government for all graduate and professional students. To me she seemed self-assured and focused, but clearly her adviser's lack of interest had eroded her confidence. The adviser's undermining treatment began early on. "I took my qualifying exams (an important step in the Ph.D. process) early, and his only remark was 'I'm surprised you passed!' I wasn't sure if he was surprised because I am a woman, or because I am black." (Lola was born in Nigeria and came to the United States when she was seventeen.) In the lab, Lola says, her adviser picked clear favorites and marginalized female graduate students.

But Lola's story has a happy ending. She found a mentor in the Business School, an informal adviser who encouraged her to explore a new field of interest—international policy, where she will be able to make use of her scientific background—and is helping her redirect her career to positions in Washington, D.C.

In my own case, a mentor, a male history professor at Vassar, encouraged me to seek a career of my own. At the time I didn't see him as a role model— he was a graying old man and a mediocre teacher—but he opened my mind to new possibilities. The women professors I met at Vassar (many of them distinguished and authoritative) should have been my role models; they were the first professional women I had ever encountered, growing up as I did in small towns in northern Minnesota. I was in awe of them, but they had two characteristics that precluded them from serving as role models: they were old and they were unmarried.

Even when I insisted on putting my wedding and husband's career before my own ambitions, my mentor at Vassar urged me to consider an academic career in history, ultimately as a university professor. He brought to my attention various prestigious fellowships I could apply for and said he was confident I would secure one. And in spite of my reluctance, he continued to persuade me to think beyond my family plans and pursue a more ambitious career path.

Somehow his persistence won me over. I married in July, three weeks after graduation, set up house in married student apartments at my husband's university, and enrolled in a history Ph.D. program, fellowship in hand. Thanks to a mentor, I made the decision to pursue both a career and a marriage—an assertive choice for the era, and not one well appreciated by my family or peers.

Interestingly, mothers too often serve as motivating figures. For example, Lynn Pontin, an adolescent psychiatry professor, chose her career path partly in response to her mother's deferred ambitions. Lynn's parents met in law school but her mother dropped out to raise kids and became a teacher as a backup plan. "[My mother] was very negative about never practicing and it was a major factor in me being determined to have a career and have it run at full tilt so I would not feel I was sacrificing so much for my children."

Alice Agogino, a mechanical engineering professor at Berkeley, chose her career path in part because of her mother's difficult struggle. A physics professor at Eastern New Mexico University during Alice's high school years, her mother was one of a very few women physicists in postwar America. She faced institutional sexism throughout her career but did not acknowledge the structural barriers she confronted. "My mother was working for a rocket design company and was the head of fifteen engineers. At the time, they had no females in positions of power as managers or engineers, and even though she was the head of fifteen engineers, she got half of their salary, and she had no friends. At the time, she denied any discrimination but it was obviously occurring; it's a phenomenon that occurs to women early in the field."

When Alice ultimately chose to study engineering, she drew on the lessons learned from her mother's insistence on having the right to have a career and her struggle for recognition from her colleagues. That belief system helped her handle the gender bias she encountered in graduate school as one of few women in the engineering department. "I walked into the first class, a drafting class, and as I entered the room the instructor looked at me and said, 'Oh, there's a woman in the class so we can't tell any jokes.' I frankly did not know there weren't any women in the program or in the field—it was a shock but it definitely galvanized me."

Alice is now a professor of mechanical engineering at Berkeley with a distinguished record of achievement (she was elected to the National Academy of Engineers at an exceptionally young age). While getting her degree in chemical engineering, she had a baby and graduated at the top of her class—at the age of twenty-one.

According to Alice even small, symbolic gestures can make a difference in attracting women to the field. "I fought for fifteen years to take down these photographs of fifty men that were on the walls of the department. I did not make a stink the first year, but those photos really did get to me. I started working with student groups and got $70,000 worth of money to help graduate women and to get the photos taken down; to create an environment and a climate appropriate for women."

Thanks to women like Alice, girls today have more role models. There is a woman on the Supreme Court, a handful of women senators, and even more congresswomen, including the current Speaker of the House. Young women today have grown accustomed to women doctors and women lawyers, and may perhaps have them in their own families. About 30 percent of all practicing lawyers and 25 percent of doctors of all ages are now women, and this figure ramps up to about 50 percent of the new graduating crop.[23] Highly visible women in powerful roles prove to younger generations that having it all is possible.

MAKING THE CASE FOR STUDENT PARENTS

Family concerns clearly affect women's choices and paths during the student years. Yet there remains a great disconnect between the feminization of professional education and the adoption of family-friendly policies for graduate students. A recent article in the *New York Times* points to the many changes that the feminization of professional education has wrought. According to the author, "business students network at potluck dinners, medical schools incorporate more materials on women's health. At law schools, the Socratic method has come under attack, its dominance diluted by approaches thought to be more women friendly." The article points to the difference Elena Kagan, the first woman dean of Harvard Law School, has made. Within her first few months in office she made sure that free tampons were available in every women's bathroom in Harvard Law School. "It's such a small thing, but it says a lot about whether a place cares about women," she said.[24]

Still, these small steps are unlikely to provide a large step forward in changing the culture. A great void in this description of the feminization of professional education is any mention of children or spouses. One would expect that the newly realized high density of women would prompt family-friendly innovations like child care or an extended academic plan, and there are signs that fundamental change is not only possible but also achievable. The student years should be a good time to start a family, offering young parents the advantages of a flexible schedule and strong community. According to Anna Westerstahl Stenport, a Berkeley graduate student who gave birth to a daughter while working on her doctorate, having a child during one's student years can make a lot of economic sense. The university offers family housing and subsidized early childhood care. Berkeley recently opened a new infant and toddler care center where graduate students' children are allotted a generous proportion of the coveted slots.

Anna says her student schedule meshed fairly well with motherhood. She worked forty-five to fifty hours a week, but these hours were flexible. Having a committed partner willing to share the parenting workload was crucial; Anna's husband had a work schedule that permitted him to take care of Marta when she couldn't.

Anna's faculty adviser had a five-year-old daughter and completely supported her maternity. I asked if she thought her family might be an impediment in the job market. "Not right now, right here, but when I went to the job fair for the Modern Language Association [for job interviews] last November, I did not wear my wedding band nor did I bring up my family."

Time passed. I heard from Anna again about a year after her interview at the Modern Language Association. "You will be happy to know," she said triumphantly, "that I got a job at [a major research university], and I was pregnant at the time of the interview. Guess what? They offered me my first semester off for parental leave!" This was indeed a happy outcome for this student parent, and a hopeful sign that the culture is inching forward toward family friendliness.

Student life, as Anna relates, can offer a fairly nurturing environment for young mothers. Our university, like many others, stops the clock for student parents. They are allowed to leave for a semester and return without penalty. We also offer a substantial grant to help student parents with their child raising costs. Yale University has pioneered a five-year medical school plan for student parents who wish to withdraw for a year. There are indications that attitudes are changing as well. At a recent faculty meeting, a distinguished senior scientist took me aside and proudly announced that two of his students were pregnant. He assured me that this would not hinder their careers, and that he had organized a baby shower for them.

Our research shows that women who had children during graduate school or within five years afterward and continued in their careers had as high a success rate as women without children.[25] Not taking a break proved to be a successful strategy. And, as we shall see, the increasing number of family accommodations at universities, corporations, and other institutions allow more mothers to continue their careers without a lengthy interruption or detour into a second tier.

Some universities are also working to address the two body problem, an additional family–career juncture that can derail highly qualified women from the fast track. Several institutions now offer the spouses of sought-after candidates jobs as well. They have recognized the downside of hiring one partner and not the other—professors who are separated from their spouses typically aren't happy and are often less productive. Couples who live and work together are more likely to be stable, successful participants in their campus communities.

These examples prove that although challenging, implementing family-friendly policies *is* possible. The structure of the workplace—be it a corporate office or university research lab—*can* be altered. In our experience at Berkeley, these reforms have improved our competitive edge and allowed us to attract the best talent to our institution. Other universities are taking similar steps as they compete for the best candidates. Ultimately family-friendly policies will become the accepted norm.

3

The Make-or-Break Years:
Thirty to Forty

Young women don't want to be identified as feminists even
if they agree with the specifics of the movement—whereas
our generation is proud to be called feminist because it
was such a life changing movement for us. I don't want to
denigrate the next generation that wants to spend more time
at home with their children. However for those who stop
working altogether, how long you stay out of the workforce
is crucial: More than two years out and it becomes harder
to get back in.
—Lynn Povich, former editor in chief, *Working Woman*

The decade between thirty and forty is when women today make the hardest
choices: whether to seek a fast track position after securing their degree;
whether to have a child; whether to stay on the fast track after having a child
or to leave the race and find a less competitive role. They face new and for-
midable challenges, and there are rarely second chances if they opt out.

Not surprisingly, this is the decade when the career and family trajectories
of men and women distinctly diverge. Many women leave the fast track during these years to accommodate motherhood, but few men do so for fatherhood. Men who remain on the fast track are more likely to have children than
career women. In both work and family measures, men and women are no
longer on equal footing.

BREAKING INTO THE FAST TRACK

There are now two generations of women who have faced the critical make-or-
break decade that determines the rest of their career life. The first generation,

the pioneers, confronted a male-dominated, often hostile workplace. During their make-or-break years they forced their way through closed doors by means of lawsuits, collective action, and determination. Women fought these battles to secure a place at the bargaining table, but their progress fell short of remaking the workplace into a family-friendly environment. The next generation encountered fewer barriers but faced a workplace that is faster and ever more demanding. The challenge of this generation is to change the structure of the workplace.

THE FIRST WAVE OF CAREER WOMEN

"Have you noticed—there are no women here over forty?" my daughter Eve commented as we entered the elegant Frank Gehry–designed cafeteria located in the Conde Nast building on Times Square. This skyscraper houses many of the nation's most influential magazines: *New Yorker, Vogue, Gentlemen's Quarterly, Architectural Digest*. For aspiring journalists and photographers it is the "mothership." Nearly everyone in the industry has submitted to, and likely been rejected by, at least one magazine at this address.

My daughter was right. Looking around the glass-walled, beautifully appointed cafeteria, I noticed that everyone appeared very young and there were many more women than men. Most were dressed in casual business attire, with a strong emphasis on black. Upon closer examination I did note a few older diners—all men.

I asked Eve, then a photo assistant at *GQ*, if she thought any of these women were mothers. "Not a chance," she said. The media world, publishing and broadcast, is run by the young, and particularly by young women. There is no formal academic training period as there is for doctors, lawyers, and academics. Young workers begin as apprentices, performing whatever grunt work they are assigned while slowly moving up toward junior editorships. The probationary period is both earlier and longer. At the top of this pyramid are a few choice positions, usually occupied by men. Still there are a noteworthy number of women editors in chief, more than in other corporate structures; a full 18 percent of top executives in publishing are women.[1]

This accomplishment is attributable in large part to three decades of political pressure and several lawsuits, which helped open up opportunities for women in management and senior editorial positions. Lynn Povich, former

editor in chief of *Working Woman* magazine, was a major player in a seminal
sex discrimination lawsuit against *Newsweek* in 1970. "In the summer of '69
Newsweek asked me to begin reporting on the women's movement since I
was the only woman writer on the magazine at the time. All the other women
were researchers or reporters. I would return to the office and realize that we
needed to bring the movement home to *Newsweek*."

Lynn joined a small group of women at *Newsweek* who had already banded
together to do something decisive. They understood the firmly entrenched
hierarchy of the publication and knew that collective legal action would be the
best way to force true change. The women had difficulty finding a female lawyer
(most women practiced in estates and trust law at the time) but eventually
Eleanor Holmes Norton, a lawyer with New York ACLU who is now the congresswoman for the District of Columbia, took the case. Norton took one look
at the magazine's masthead, with men from the top down to the bottom category and women only at the bottom rung, and realized there was a pattern
of discrimination. "By the end of 1969 the women's movement was getting so
big that *Newsweek* decided they had to write a cover story on it; on March 16,
1970, the magazine appeared on the newsstands with a cover story titled
'Women in Revolt' and 46 female staffers announced their lawsuit on the same
day. We knew the publicity would get them more than anything else," Lynn
recalled.

The story of the first sex discrimination suit by women in the media was
picked up across the country and around the world. After months of negotiations with editors, a memorandum of understanding was signed that
August. But two years later the women were so dissatisfied with the lack of
progress that they sued again. "This time we created goals and timetables to
have a third of the writers and reporters be women and a third of fact check-
ers be men so that the job wouldn't be viewed as a 'woman's job.' The final
request was to have a female senior editor appointed by the end of 1975.
There was resistance to having a female in management but the women
persisted."

Lynn was appointed *Newsweek*'s first female senior editor in August 1975.

Now, more than thirty years later, Lynn sees progress but not victory. She
had hoped that once enough women were in the career pipeline, the management structure would shift toward gender balance. "What is being asked
of people in the workplace is often more than women feel is worth it. They
are still being discriminated against at certain levels. However, I think the

discrimination is much less—it's the workplace culture that has not changed enough."

Similar patterns typify the world of corporate law. Peek into any partners' lounge in a major law firm and the attorneys stopping by for coffee or soft drinks are likely to be men over forty. Among the small trickle of women who venture in, only a handful will be over forty; fewer than 17 percent of partners in large firms are women.[2]

As in the publishing world, the fact that there are any women at all in management is a testament to the drive of the pioneer generation. Maryellen Herringer, the first woman partner in a major San Francisco law firm, was one of a handful of women who graduated from Boalt Hall in 1968.

Initially unable to find work as a lawyer in San Francisco, where firms made it clear that women need not apply, she moved to New York and found a job with a well-known Wall Street law firm, Davis, Polk & Wardwell. New York, unlike San Francisco at the time, already had a visible presence of women practicing in some of the larger firms. During World War II the absence of men had forced these firms, the largest in the country, to use female lawyers, and the tradition continued after the war ended. By the fall of 1969, Maryellen discerned a palpable change in attitudes in San Francisco law firms. She accepted a position at Orrick, Herrington & Sutcliff and became the first female lawyer in that office. She learned later that she had obtained this position by the luck of good timing. "The hiring partner had been opposed to female lawyers. His point of view was that you hire them, you train them, and then they leave you to go have children. But he was in the hospital the week they hired me."

At the time of her hire, there were a total of three other women in all of the large San Francisco law firms. Despite the daunting odds, Maryellen received a great deal of support from the well-established lawyers in her firm. During her first weeks on the job, one senior practicing lawyer said, "It ain't easy to be Jackie Robinson; how can I help?"

But the overall climate of the law firm was chilly toward women. "There were many incidents of many kinds in and outside the office. In the office I was hit on and treated in a condescending way. People would make jokes all the time, and sometimes you live with it and sometimes you challenge them. Early on I was assigned to a case and the client did not want a woman on the account. The firm stood by me and stated 'if you want us to be your law firm then you have to respect our decision to have her as your lawyer.'" The client kept her on and ended up approving of her work. Maryellen describes the experience with good humor: "It's like a dog who can talk—they were quite amazed once I proved myself."

Maryellen's rise to partnership in 1975 did not reflect a sudden change of heart in the legal world. It took many individual battles and a famous Supreme Court decision to challenge the "men's club" and fully open the doors.

One of those battles was Elizabeth Anderson Hishon's. In 1972 Hishon accepted a position as an associate at a large established Atlanta law firm with fifty male partners that had been notoriously closed to female partners. Hishon claimed that the promise of ultimate partnership was a recruiting device to induce her and other young lawyers to become associates at the firm. Advancement to partnership after five or more years was "a matter of course" for associates "who received satisfactory evaluations," she claimed. Hishon received satisfactory evaluations, but when partnership decisions occurred, she was rejected and asked to leave while many of her male peers were offered partnerships.

Hishon brought a sex discrimination suit under Title VII of the Civil Rights Act of 1964. She was turned away by a federal district court and again by a federal appeals court, which sided with the law firm that partnership decisions were a private matter. Finally, in 1984, the U.S. Supreme Court agreed to hear the case and, to the surprise of many, sided with Hishon in her claim that indeed consideration for partnership was one of the "terms, conditions, or privileges of employment" intended by Title VII.[3]

Hishon did not automatically win a partnership slot, but she won her day in court. Hishon's victory was a day of celebration for the professional women's associations that had joined in the lawsuit. Women now had the right to work and succeed in all law firms and, by extension, most other employment situations where women were denied promotions on the basis of their sex.

Several decades later, this legal victory has transformed the hiring and promotion practices of law firms. Yet, as in the publishing world, young women aren't assuming their place among the top positions in these firms and instead tend to dominate the lower rungs of the corporate structure. Most of the discriminatory barriers have been removed, but the workplace environment remains the same. *More Than Part Time,* a study focusing on Massachusetts firms, reveals that the attrition rate for women attorneys is about 70 percent higher than the attrition rate for male attorneys.[4]

THE PROBATIONARY PERIOD

The victories of the women's movement have been tempered by the fact that the structure of the fast track remains essentially unchanged, and decidedly family unfriendly. In fact, there is evidence that the game has become even more difficult; the push for more billable hours, more publications, and ever longer workweeks have gradually sped up the already taxing fast track.

According to demographers Jerry Jacobs and Kathleen Gerson, the professional and managerial classes in America are working longer hours than they did in 1970, while other classes of workers are working less. The biggest change is in the number of hours worked by women who have poured into these higher occupational strata. The percentage of women who work more than fifty hours a week has more than doubled.[5]

In all high-powered professions the make-or-break period is the proving ground for future career success. There is little tolerance for mediocrity during these years; only excellence is rewarded. Standards of excellence vary across the professions, but they all require a great deal of hard work. The nature of the work is different from the student years; now there are strict time schedules and, in some professions like law, there are billable hours which require timekeeping to the minute. The level of responsibility is much greater. If one fails at an important task, it's not just a personal failure; there are patients, clients, students, shareholders, and employees to contend with.

MAKING PARTNER

In the legal world the race to partnership, a track stretching from five to ten years, defines the probationary period for most ambitious young lawyers. The new associate, under the supervision of a partner, must put in a working week of billable hours, usually performing drudge work and in addition, an unspecified number of hours of networking with clients and partners to prove he or she is partnership material.

The great majority of lawyers—75 percent of all men and 71 percent of all women—practice law in private law firms.[6] Private firms range from solo practitioners to megafirms of more than a thousand lawyers in several cities and sometimes several countries. Women have entered the legal profession in large numbers at a time of immense change. The pace of work at private firms has greatly accelerated over the past thirty years and expectations of productivity, measured by billable hours, have risen. Firms that were literally "men's clubs" thirty years ago are now large corporate structures.

Carole C., a young attorney on the partnership track in a major San Francisco law firm, confides that her father, also a lawyer, tried to dissuade her from a law career due to these changes. "When he started out, it was more of a profession with regular hours and there wasn't the constant drive to bill more hours and work harder and harder. It gradually became more of a business operated on a business model."

Still, the rewards are greater than ever before, with partners' salaries escalating well beyond what Carole's father's generation could expect. And as law firms become more global, the nature of the work has grown more complex—and more interesting.

The large firms offer the highest prestige and greatest rewards and also serve as the springboard to important government positions and federal judgeships. Women, however, account for only about 16 percent of partners in these large law firms.[7] Although men and women enter the track to partnership at roughly the same rate, a 2001 American Bar Association report reveals that men are at least twice as likely as similarly qualified women to achieve partnership.[8] Most research on the high attrition rate among female lawyers does not attempt to explain the huge exodus; it's as if researchers are afraid to revive the old debates on why women are different. But the Boston Bar Association Task Force on Professional Challenges and Family Needs found that, at least in Massachusetts law firms, the major reason for women's attrition is "family–life balance concerns."[9]

Men fall off the partnership track at high rates as well. With the accelerated pace of legal careers, the fast track has become an increasingly slippery track. A majority of junior associates do not make it through the probationary period.[10] Still, men are far less likely than women to exit the partnership track, and those who leave do not cite family reasons. This may mean that men, in a culture where male identity is tied to the breadwinning ability, are simply unwilling to admit that family is a priority.

There are key elements to successfully passing this probationary period on the road to partnership. First, a junior associate must demonstrate a willingness to work long hours. Second, the young lawyer must demonstrate an ability to work on tough, career-defining cases. Third, a young attorney should establish a mentor relationship with a senior partner. And finally, an associate must network, which is crucial to the future of any attorney who wishes to make it to partner.[11]

These rigorous requirements naturally disadvantage lawyers with significant family responsibilities. Not only do junior associate parents have difficulty working extremely long hours (sixty-plus hour workweeks are the norm), they do not have time to engage in after-hours networking. Time constraints also influence whether an associate can tackle a high profile, high-demand case, and whether a senior attorney believes it is worth his time to mentor a young attorney who has divided commitments.

Ann, now a young mother who left the partnership track as a litigator shortly after her wedding, commented, "It was fun at first, the deadlines, the excitement. I liked practicing law, I thought I loved practicing law. Steve [Ann's husband] was also a litigator and before we were married, we could talk about our work and understand when one of us had to work over the weekend to file a complaint or whatever. I guess it stopped being fun when we were planning our wedding and I couldn't even spend time with my family who came across the country because another deadline came up. I don't like to be a quitter. And I still have some regrets. I wish I had organized my life better."

I asked Ashley Dunning, now a partner in a major law firm who waited until becoming a partner before having a child, why she thought so many women dropped out of the fast track. "The women attorneys I have observed generally set exceptionally high standards for themselves in all aspects of their lives, through school, in their careers, and their personal lives. They juggle a lot. Becoming a mother can throw their lives (and particularly their career goals) into, often temporary, disarray because first they've gone through the physical drain of the pregnancy and now have the awesome responsibility of caring for an infant, and they set a very high standard for themselves in that most demanding role too. The long term responsibility of parenthood also impacts how they perceive their career opportunities. When a law firm does not provide the flexibility that is required for parents (and more often mothers) to meet those competing demands, women will sometimes opt out entirely from the job, rather than trying to work it out. The longer term perspective that I believe would benefit both law firm managers and the women attorneys facing this dilemma is that they may both be better off for making some adjustments so as to work it out. At the end of the day, the woman will not feel like she's compromised all of her professional goals for her children, and the law firm will benefit from having experienced, savvy women in their senior ranks."

Maryellen Herringer, the first female partner in her major San Francisco law firm, also deferred motherhood, but not entirely by choice. Maryellen was married three years after achieving partnership but was at first unable to conceive. Not having children gave her freedom to work long hours.

One of her clients, the Transamerica Corporation of San Francisco, offered her a position as general counsel. After initially declining, she accepted in 1981 after a new CEO came in. Though there were other women in management, Maryellen made her way to become the corporation's first woman senior vice president.

At age forty-two, Maryellen gave birth to her first child. By any standards, she was accomplished and well established in her career, but this did not afford her any special treatment for maternity leave. She returned three weeks after childbirth because she was needed at the office. Though the hours were more standard and humane as general counsel in comparison to private practice, there were limitations. "When you are in a company, if they are doing a transaction, you have got to be there no matter how inconvenient it is for you. At a law firm, it's possible to find flexibility with people who can fill in for you."

Her second child was born six years later, when she was forty-eight. To manage the household responsibilities, Maryellen and her husband had two nannies—a day nanny from 7:00 A.M. to 7:00 P.M., then a night nanny 7:00 P.M. to 9:00 P.M. and weekends.

Deferring motherhood is a risky game. Few women are likely to have children late into their forties as Maryellen did. Many women are sorry about this choice. Thirty-eight percent of UC faculty women (compared with 11 percent of men) reported that they regretted not having more children. This included women who had none at all.[12]

MAKING IT IN MEDICINE

The residency following medical school is both a continuation of the training period and a first job. Because the residency is a hybrid between schooling and employment, residents attend to patients but are paid much less than senior doctors. This period generally stretches from four to seven or more years depending on the specialization, and the work is famously grueling, a fact that came to light on a March night in 1984. On that night a young woman, Libby Zion, came to the emergency room of a New York hospital complaining of a fever and died eight hours later. Her family sued the hospital for malpractice, and in the course of the lawsuit, the working conditions of medical residents became known to the public.

The family attorney argued that there was only one explanation for why the first-year medical resident neither came to Zion's side nor called for a supervisor's help when nurses warned that the patient was thrashing wildly. The system had put the sleep-deprived doctor, "practically a zombie," in charge of more than forty patients. It was revealed that medical residents routinely worked more than eighty hours a week, usually in shifts of more than thirty hours each.

In part as a reaction to public alarm provoked by the lawsuit, New York passed the first law in the nation limiting the workweek of residents to eighty hours with maximum shifts of twenty-four hours. That was considered great progress in a world where many residents were working more than 100 hours a week, sometimes even 120 hours, often for thirty-six-hour stretches at a time.

A survey taken over ten years later found that more than half of the teaching hospitals inspected by the state Health Department had violated state laws meant to ensure that medical residents are not exhausted when caring for patients. Thirty of the fifty-four hospitals in violation were in New York City.[13] The legal limit nationally is now set at eighty hours per week, but some specialties, like surgery, are excepted from this rule and enforcement is spotty.[14]

Medicine offers a phenomenal example of increased access to a male-dominated profession. The proportion of women in U.S. medical schools has risen from less than 10 percent prior to 1970 to nearly 46 percent today.[15] In 1998 Yale, Harvard, UCSF, and Johns Hopkins medical schools had graduating classes of over 50 percent women. Residencies are currently composed of nearly 35 percent female residents, and the AMA predicts that one-third of all physicians will be women by the year 2010.[16]

While residencies can be considered a probationary period and usually fall during the make-or-break years when residents are in their thirties, they are not structured as an "up or out" system like the partnership track for lawyers and tenure track for professors. The work schedule is demanding, but at the end of the residency there will be a job for everyone. Because of their age, about half of women doctors have their first child while residents. According to Karie Frasch, whose partner, Barb, is an emergency room resident, in a hectic setting probably not that much different than the one Libby Zion entered more then twenty years ago, "the schedule is insane, but there is still a baby boom. All residents get four weeks off a year on the rotation and they plan ahead. If they need more time, they have to make it up at the end. They help each other a lot. And I think they can see the end in sight." The light at the end of the residency tunnel is possibility of a far more flexible schedule in emergency medicine, and a bump in salary from about $50,000 to $150,000.

Overall, women doctors are only slightly less likely than men to drop out of the profession (5 percent).[17] This is a much lower attrition rate than law, academia, or any other of the male-dominated fast track professions. But while female residents tend to stay the course, they often pursue a less demanding specialty. They are likely to enter primary care, where the hours are more flexible, and much less likely to enter a higher status, higher paying surgery residency; only about 4 percent of surgeons are women.[18] Academic medicine (joining the faculty of a medical school) is also remarkably absent of women. Choosing this path requires facing yet another major hurdle—a seven-year effort to achieve tenure, which is ultimately based on the candidate's success with publishing in academic journals. Positions with top medical schools, the centers of cutting-edge research, are considered by most to be the top of profession. The doctors in these positions are most likely to make the breakthrough discoveries that determine new clinical directions that shape the profession. Tenure track in medical schools includes teaching, research, and usually, except for the strict research positions, seeing patients as well. These hardy doctors are enduring, in effect, their second probationary period. A successful acolyte is likely to be over forty when the tenure prize is won. Only 11 percent of full professors in medical schools are women,[19] and today with even numbers of men and women in medicine, only roughly 26 percent of academic medicine professors are women.[20] More telling, only 7.5 percent of department chairs, a powerful position in the medical establishment, are women, while only approximately 3 percent of deans are women.[21] Medical schools are relentlessly hierarchical, some would say feudal, and the feudal lords are all men. Chairs and deans, far more than in universities, wield ultimate power over salaries, appointments, and space—the infrastructure for a successful career. Until recently, there was no welcoming hand reaching out to women and minorities. It's not surprising that, in this highly authoritarian environment, the chilly climate has dissuaded women from applying.

Whether they have actively chosen these primary care specialties or, as in the sciences and engineering, they have been discouraged from pursuing the rigors of surgery or academic medicine is a matter of active debate. It's clear that workforce shortages also play a role: the nation needs more primary care physicians than it does specialists. In 1992 the Council on Graduate Medical Education set a national goal for at least half of med school graduates to begin careers in family practice, general internal medicine, or general pediatrics by the year 2000. Now, well into the twenty-first century, this goal is being approached.[22]

This topsy-turvy distribution, with many more women in primary care and many more men in surgery, is based on the choices that women make in medical school. As they rotate through specialty training, students have an opportunity to view the work life of most doctors. They can see that surgeons are mostly male, they work dauntingly long hours, they are constantly on call, and their residencies last at least seven years. They can also see that there are far more women doctors in primary care specialties and that the residency is usually three or four years.

Still, medicine overall offers better options than the other professions for balancing family life, particularly outside academic medicine. Women doctors are more likely to have children than women in any other fast track profession, a topic that will be discussed in subsequent sections. Female physicians are also more likely to be married than their counterparts in other demanding careers.

Like law, medicine is undergoing a revolution in its delivery of services. The relentless takeover by HMOs is quickly transforming doctors from once independent professionals to corporate employees.[23] The dark side of this trend is the erosion of physicians' status, pay, and autonomy. The bright side, particularly for mothers, is the increasing ability to choose their own work schedule, work three days a week rather than five or thirty hours rather than fifty, and still enjoy relatively high wages and satisfying work. Without much notice, the medical profession is leading the way in the feminization of male-dominated professions.

CAPTURING THE GOLDEN RING OF TENURE

The university world, like law, requires an intense, clearly defined "up or out" probationary period. Unlike most professions, those who do not make the grade must find employment elsewhere. This may be employment within the profession, but it is unlikely to be at the same level of status and income. It may be at a lesser university or junior college, or it may be a part-time or adjunct position.

The average assistant professor is in his or her early thirties when hired. Candidates have spent five to seven years securing a Ph.D. and increasingly, in many sciences, a few years more on a postdoctoral fellowship.[24]

The ivory tower is not a peaceful oasis. The road to tenure can last up to nine pressure cooker years for all young professors. The race to publish in peer-reviewed journals is unrelenting and with tenuous job security, new faculty are under daily pressure to prove that they are good teachers, good citizens in the department, but, most of all, that they have the "right stuff" to become academic stars. When the time comes for deciding the fate of the assistant professor, usually after six years and at around age forty, a closed procedure occurs in which his or her publications are carefully scrutinized at several anonymous levels within the university and without. The process can be agonizingly long and the result, if negative, a crushing defeat. Young professors who are not granted tenure must leave the university entirely; they are offered no comfortable career plateau.

A colleague of mine, now a full professor in political science, recounted his first years. "The first two years I had to teach four new courses, two of which I had never studied myself. One class was a large lecture, three hundred students, with six TAs. I'll bet I spent fifty hours a week just on that course, and at the end the students gave me evaluations that truly stank. It got better, but at the end of two years I had only written about twenty pages; I still had a book and three articles to complete for tenure."

Women assistant professors are far less likely than men to be parents when hired.[25] As noted in Chapter 2, women students are afraid of being taken less seriously if they have a baby, and mothers tend to delay or defer taking on this first daunting job. Mothers with Ph.D.'s are less likely to take on challenging university entry-level positions; they are in the "first cut" that separates men and women in their career trajectories. Many mothers and married women intending to become mothers have already determined that the rigors of the tenure process and the demanding career beyond it are more than they are willing to take on. Single women, on the other hand, land that first job in the same numbers that men do.[26]

There are no billable hours in the university world. Merit is measured by productivity, not time, and assistant professors tend to put in long hours in order to meet departmental expectations. The flexible time arrangement still creates challenges for working parents. Mothers are less likely to travel to attend conferences to present their research findings to other scholars—a critical step in career advancement.[27]

Science and engineering present particular challenges. As noted in Chapter 2, the pool is already shallow. Relatively few women receive Ph.D.'s in the physical sciences and engineering, and that number dwindles with entry into the first university positions. Many women have already chosen to enter industry, which they perceive to be less competitive and to offer more controllable hours. And, in general, the university world has been slow to accept mothers in science.

Angelica Stacy, a distinguished professor of chemistry, recalls bringing her newborn child and her mother (as baby-sitter) to a scientific conference fifteen years go: "There was no child care, there were no children, and, in fact, there were very few women. They threw my mother and my baby out of the conference. They said it was unprecedented."

For many academic mothers, such barriers represent real obstacles to career advancement. Scientific conferences are important venues for career networking and garnering attention for research. Women who don't attend conferences for family reasons miss out on membership on national committees, the opportunity to attract essential funding, and the chance to personally connect with other influential players in their field. And federal grants, the financial bedrock support for most scientific research, offer no accommodation for childbirth.

Dr. Renee Binder, professor of psychiatry, says she advises new academic mothers who are still assistant professors to maintain some connections but not to let professional obligations become overwhelming. "You want to keep your finger in [committee work]; you don't want to become president of an association when you have a one-year-old; that's just crazy. When I got called from a nominating committee to head something I would say, 'My kids are little but I am interested; please keep my name in mind for the future.'"

Keeping connected to the network is essential. The tenure clock does not stop or does not stop for long (some universities allow an extra year for childbirth). Failing to play the networking game can seriously impede a mother's chance for obtaining tenure.

At the finish line of the tenure race, the winners are likely to be men with children and the losers women with children. Our Do Babies Matter? research team studied the careers of 160,000 through retirement. The most startling finding is that men with children were 38 percent more likely than married women with children to achieve tenure but also somewhat better than single men. A large percentage of mothers fell into the second tier—the part-time, adjunct, nontenure track. Single women and married women without children fell behind men with children but were far more competitive than mothers.[28] As across all the professions, married men with children led the career pack and married women with children lagged far behind or fell off the track.

With the huge growth of women in the Ph.D. pool, there are far more women on faculties today than there were thirty years ago. At Berkeley and other major research universities, women comprise close to 25 percent of the faculty, while in 1970 that figure was 2.5 percent. The numbers are slowly rising, but there is a cost. A high percentage of these women faculty, as we shall see, are not mothers.

ESTABLISHING A VOICE IN THE MEDIA

The media world encompasses a wide variety of communications enterprises—from books and newspapers to television, radio, and advertising—all designed to inform the public and influence public opinion. Arguably, they are collectively the most influential voice in our society. Women are attracted to this world in large numbers and flood to the centers of power—mainly New York and a few other large cities. These young women in their twenties are numerous in the lower ranks; they are the copy editors, the news researchers, and the advertising design assistants. However, their numbers thin out dramatically as they reach their thirties.

By definition, the media world runs on deadlines, and in the news industry, these deadlines are determined by breaking events. News, not family, must rule the aspiring executive's schedule. Missie Rennie, a former executive producer at CBS News with two grown children, reflects on the television industry. "You never know when news is going to happen. You don't know that Rabin will be assassinated on a certain day when possibly you have other plans for the next day. You plan the shows during the week but the complexion can change overnight."

There is a probationary period when young women and men strive to break through the glass ceiling of middle management into senior positions, but that breakthrough does not offer greater control of time. Everyone involved in putting on a newscast, from the cameraman to the producer, has to be in the studio when news happens. "Television is also unique in that it is all about teamwork. You cannot be in control and get a show on the air unless the director, the producer, and the person writing the tiny font are all in synch in order for the product to work. When news happens everyone is there from vice president all the way down," notes Rennie.

The Annenberg Public Policy Center monitors the progress of women in the communications industry. It watches the telecom, print publishing, and advertising companies that are among the Fortune 500—the New York Times, AT&T, McGraw-Hill, and Grey Global, and other big players.[29] The communications industry, like all of the Fortune 500 elite, is still largely an old boys' club. Overall, women comprise 15 percent of executive leaders, a static proportion that has changed little in recent years, and 12 percent of board members in the top communications companies.

Some parts of the industry are far more welcoming than others; publishing companies boast a relatively robust 18 percent women executives and the same percentage on their corporate boards, the powerful governing group that determines the direction of the corporation. Advertising firms, on the other hand, have made little progress toward gender equality; in these firms women hold a spare 3 percent of executive positions and only 9 percent of chairs on corporate boards.[30]

The important but often overlooked story is that women are stuck in the amorphous middle management positions—the junior editors, personnel managers, copy chiefs—accounting for 41 percent of all management positions among communications companies.[31] These are the positions just below the infamous first glass ceiling of senior manager—producer, director, senior editor—and well below the second glass ceiling of editors in chief and

CEOs. There is no "up or out" policy, as there is with gaining partnership for lawyers and tenure for professors. Those who do not move up can languish in low to midlevel management for their career life, a relatively comfortable plateau. A break through the first glass ceiling to senior management is likely to occur, if at all, during the make-or-break years, when young workers are in their thirties.

However, rising to senior management does not offer real job security in this world. A seasoned professional gains respect, experience, and reputation over time and can move to more prestigious positions, but even old familiar faces on television can be terminated without notice.

Missie Rennie quoted a longtime friend, an anchorwoman, who described the nature of the TV industry job security this way: "You're fine, you're fine, you're fine, you're fired." According to Rennie the standard is three- to five-year contracts that give a certain degree of stability. But she points out that there is a movement toward hiring more freelancers who have flexibility but no job security.

CLIMBING THE CORPORATE LADDER

Many aspire to climb the corporate ladder to the most powerful positions in business—executive positions with Fortune 500 companies. The decision makers who head these powerful organizations are recognized as our modern captains of industry. They are paid millions of dollars in annual compensation and they wield great power—over their corporations, over the national economy, and increasingly over the global market. Fortune 500 industries are steeply pyramidal, and at the top of the pyramid there are almost no women. In America, only seven Fortune 500 CEOs are female.[32]

The fierce competition and the hefty rewards begin early. Newly minted MBAs can expect to earn a generous salary upon graduation. The Graduate Management Admission Council reports that starting base salary for 2005 graduates was $92,000, higher with a degree from the most prestigious business schools.[33] But this payoff comes at a high personal price. These positions routinely require overtime hours and a significant sacrifice in personal time. While 53 percent of MBA students report that work–life balance issues are one of the top three factors in their first job selection, many find that their new careers do not offer this balance.[34]

Data from the MBA Alumni Perspective Survey of 2,209 MBAs reveals that 41 percent of recent graduates—those who had been working for one to five years—felt that personal and work demands were overwhelming and 37 percent said they felt that careers in business were incompatible with work–life balance.[35] Responses from the survey also suggest that in order to get ahead, MBAs correctly assume that they must put in more hours than their colleagues. MBAs who had received a promotion from their current employer by the time of the survey worked fifty-one hours per week on average, while those who had not been promoted worked forty-nine hours per week on average.[36]

Men and women are evaluated as "high potential" during these early years. By age forty, most young aspiring corporate leaders will be tagged for a future leadership or for middle management limbo.

During these make-or-break years, men climbing the corporate ladder are having children, but the burden of raising them is largely carried by wives who are not working full-time. Corporate women who have children, on the other hand, rarely have partners who remain in the home. Their husbands are also working outside the home—most of them on a fast track as well.

Women are not likely to drop out; however, they are more likely to lose steam, to get stuck. They are not breaking through the first glass ceiling in their make-or-break years. Just as in the media world, female managers in the rest of the business world are growing in number but plateauing at midlevel management positions.[37] There is no "up and out" rule, as in the university or a law firm, but there is plenty of room to become fixed near the bottom of the pyramid.

Gender discrimination is the usual suspect. There are indeed pockets of the corporate world, particularly in finance, where the climate is overtly hostile to women. A recent well-publicized federal lawsuit brought by women stockbrokers at Merrill Lynch revealed a male world where women were routinely passed over for promotions and subjected to sexual harassment. According to the arbitrator, who awarded $2.2 million to one of the plaintiffs, "Merrill's failure to train, counsel, or discipline employees who engaged in sexual harassment constitutes discrimination with malice or reckless indifference to the federally protected rights of female employees."[38]

But not all corporate environments are overtly discriminatory. Indeed, a recent study of the career progression of men and women MBAs over the course of the 1990s found that subtle forms of discrimination pervaded the workplace in the early part of the decade, but during the second half, these instances were rare. However, the study concluded, women's family situations, including periods of work interruptions and work reductions, played the most important role in holding them back.[39]

There is a silver lining to the corporate story. Many corporations, unwilling to lose some of their best talent, are implementing family-friendly policies for all workers. Some companies have taken the lead in progressive policies that already have paid off. The accounting firm Deloitte & Touche recognized in the early 1990s that women were rapidly leaking out of the partnership pipeline. They considered this a bad business result and put in place practices that encouraged women to stay with the firm. These practices extended to their corporate law department, over 40 percent of which was female. While attorneys work very hard—forty to fifty hours per week—their schedules are flexible, and they do not always have to put in face time at the office. Working at home is sometimes an option.[40] Attrition now is very low across the company. Recently the firm was singled out by the City of New York as one of the five best employers for women. It was cited as the only company to have a full suite of skills training and succession planning programs specifically for women.[41]

MAKE-OR-BREAK MOTHERHOOD

Career-minded women must endure this make-or-break decade during the decisive years for motherhood. I often hear my graduate students say, "I'll wait until I'm established in my career before having children," or "I'll think about that after I get tenure." This is the accepted wisdom of their cohort.

Still, women will have children in their thirties, if they have children at all, and they can't always afford to wait until they are established. The peak childbearing year in our studies of women professors is thirty-eight.[42] For many this coincides with their tenure year; it's also nearing the end of their fertility curve. Well-organized professors who have carefully planned to delay motherhood until they have completed the probationary period now seize the moment. That is the only year in which women faculty seriously compete in the fertility race. After that, men pull far ahead, continuing to reproduce into their forties; the baby gap widens. Men experience a second small surge of fertility in their fifties due most likely to the formation of a second family following a divorce. Women do not have that biological option.

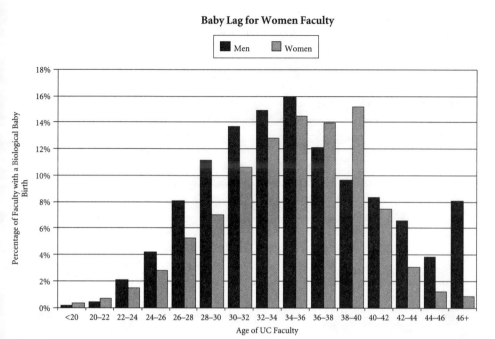

Baby Lag for Women Faculty

N = 2,809 Men
1,095 Women

The same phenomenon occurs in all fast track careers. Until their thirties, career women compete toe-to-toe with men for scholarships and awards, getting into the best graduate and professional programs, and securing the top position. Without much note, men are now pulling ahead in the fertility race.

Two factors predict whether or not a woman will have children—the first is age, the second is the number of hours spent at work. The 2000 census takers interviewed 5 percent of American households, or about 10 million people. Among the many other questions they asked each person between the ages of thirty-five and fifty was how many hours they worked each week and if they had children in their household under the age of eighteen.

The results are striking. Among professionals (doctors, lawyers, college teachers, and executives) the more hours a man works, the more likely he is to have children, while for women it is the opposite; every extra hour she works lessens her opportunity for motherhood. At the low end of the curve—those who work from one to thirty hours—82 percent of the women had children, but only 55 percent of the men did.[43] At the other end of the curve, those who worked sixty or more hours a week, 74 percent of the men had children in the household, but only 49 percent of the women did.[44]

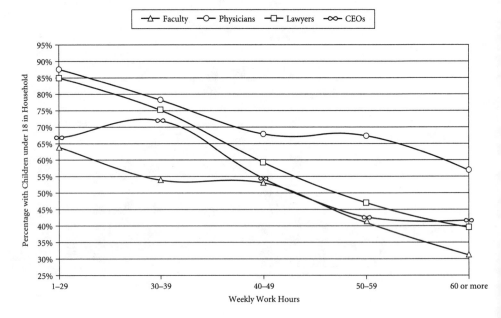

Percentage of Fast Track Women, Ages 35 to 50, with Children under 18 in the Household, by Weekly Work Hours

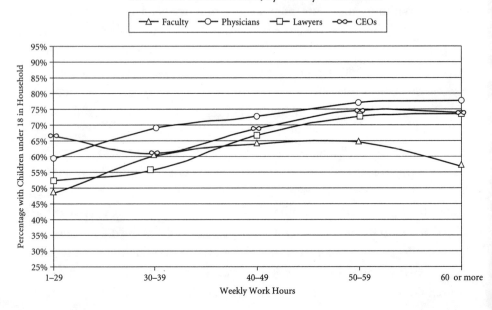

Percentage of Fast Track Men, Ages 35 to 50, with Children under 18 in the Household, by Weekly Work Hours

It is easy to understand why women who work longer are less likely to have children, but what about men? Why does their fertility increase with the number of hours they work? In part it's because men are still perceived as the primary breadwinners. In the professions, hours worked translates into economic benefits. These benefits allow men to support not only their children but also partners who do not work full-time. The evidence that this occurs is stunning. As is the case with high-level executives, male professors are far more likely to have a spouse who doesn't work than female professors are. Fifty-two percent of male professors have wives who work part-time or not at all, while only 9 percent of women professors have partners who work less than full-time.[45] For top executives the imbalance is even more striking. The largest study of global executives on work–life issues reveals that 74 percent of the women surveyed have a spouse or partner who is employed full-time, while 75 percent of men surveyed have a spouse or partner who is not employed at all.[46]

Marriage rates reveal the same paradox. The more hours a man works, the more likely he is to marry and the less likely he is to divorce. By age forty, the end of the make-or-break years, 80 to 90 percent of men, depending on their profession, will be married. Conversely, at age forty, only 58 to 70 percent of women will be married. Over the next twenty years, as men and women move into middle age, men remain firmly married, and women, with a higher divorce rate, slip slightly away from marriage.[47]

Women who begin their probationary years in law, medicine, academia, and other fast track professions have probably not examined the 2000 census, but they can look around their offices and realize that the playing field is no longer level. Men can have children and pursue their careers with full attention because they are not the primary caretakers. Some women seem able to do this as well, but they are fewer in number.

THE MEDICAL EXCEPTION

As noted, an interesting exception to this rule is the case of resident mothers. In spite of a brutal workload, half of all women doctors who have children will have their first child during their residency and 25 percent will have a second baby during this period, according to the *Journal of the American Medical Women's Association* (JAMWA).[48]

How can women residents have babies when they are working eighty-hour weeks? Indeed, why do women doctors have more babies than any other fast track professionals?[49] There are, I believe, two answers to this. As we have seen, most women do not choose the brutal surgical residencies that require at least eighty hours plus on-call duty several nights a week. Instead, women are more likely to go into the primary care specialties—OB/GYN, pediatrics, and internal medicine. Only 25 percent of surgical residents are women, while 74 percent of OB/GYN residents are women.[50] These specialties, along with psychiatry, normally require a three-year residency; the hours, although long, are less extreme.

A second reason that women can have babies during their residencies is that, particularly in the primary care specialties, there is a culture of cooperation surrounding childbirth and children. Rather than an ethos of individual competition, as exists in law, the academic world, and the corporate world, teamwork is essential throughout medicine, as it is during the residency. Members of the team can pitch in if a child is sick, a baby-sitter unavailable, or other life crises arise.

Dr. Pam Swedlow, who has just completed her residency in psychiatry at UCSF, says that the cooperative spirit among residents stems from the fact that all aspiring doctors will have jobs once they complete their training. "It is not like the academic world where it is all or nothing. There aren't the same things at stake," she said.

Motherhood is a no-nonsense business for American doctors. The American College of Obstetricians and Gynecologists advocates a six-week maternity leave for all working mothers after uncomplicated pregnancy and delivery. This period is designated as the minimum period required by a new mother to return to prepregnancy anatomy and physiology. They warn, "From the point of view of the newborn/mother/dad and other family members, secure bonding may take longer. Scandinavian countries allow physician mothers a prolonged period of paid maternity leave following each birth; Canada allows several months."[51]

JAMWA only insists on six weeks of maternity leave and recommends that "if a resident chooses to take time off exceeding that permitted by her specialty board, maternity leave policy should make provisions for the resident to make that time up at a later date." JAMWA also insists on a written policy. This tepid six-week recommendation was a bold step considering that most medical schools had no written policy and mothers had generally coped as best they could.

Residencies are indeed the stark exception to the rule; for every other fast track profession, fewer than half of female careerists are likely to have children if they work fifty hours or more each week. At the other end of the scale, the professionals who work up to thirty hours are mostly mothers (over 90 percent for women executives). Such figures suggest that the census is capturing women who have moved to part-time work or opted out after motherhood but continue to identify with their profession.

Still, there are important deviations among the professions. As noted, women doctors are more likely to have children and less likely to divorce than all others. Women professors—a class that includes medical, science, and engineering as well as history and French literature professors—perform the worst in both life arenas. Structural differences in these professions help explain this variation. While medical residencies are challenging years in terms of time demands, they are not as competitive as the probationary period in academia. And not all the other professions race the clock up to the wire. Women lawyers, if they do not delay attending law school by many years, also have the possibility of waiting for the security of partnership before age forty.

**Women Fast-Track Professionals
with Babies,* by Age**

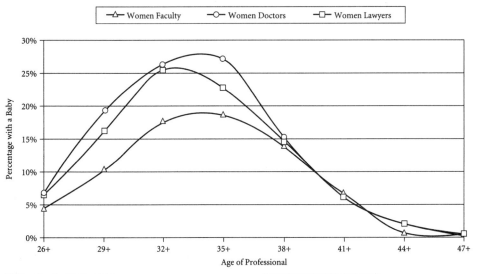

*Children, Ages 0 or 1 in Household.   *Source*: Census 2000, PUMS 5% sample.

BEST HOPES

The make-or-break years are the major challenge to both men and women across the fast track professions. Careers take off or founder during this decade. For women, all professions require a time commitment that clashes with the possibility of family formation. Although some professions continue to "eat their young," others have figured out how to integrate more flexible options into fast track career paths.

Medicine and the corporate world appear to offer the best examples. The market demand for physicians allows women to choose areas of practice— particularly primary care—where they may finally control their hours following the taxing years of residency. The corporate world, at least in some industries, is moving in the direction of offering flexible hours and work locations. Science and engineering professions in the private sector, rather than university settings, also offer more reasonable hours. And law practices now routinely offer alternatives to partnerships, some of which are becoming attractive options. Even the university world is beginning to reconsider its nineteenth-century tradition of an immutable seven-year trial period, and is beginning to stretch this venerable model to accommodate parents.

There is a cautionary tale among the promising developments, however: these alternative options may be creating a permanent second tier that will become a women's enclave, as nursing has historically been to medicine—a subject that will be explored in Chapter 5. The key to ensuring that these more flexible work arrangements become viable options for working parents is to create bridges back to the fast track so that moms and dads can continue to pursue their career ambitions once their children reach school age. How these innovative solutions will take shape and be implemented will be explored in the final chapter of this book.

4

Mothers' Choices: Staying the Course, Opting Out, or Dropping Down

> When I first went back to work, I had a little pang of guilt, which I do not think men feel, but my sister asked whether I harbor resentment for Dad for working, and I thought, no.
> —Carole C., law associate

In a radio interview, Supreme Court Justice Ruth Bader Ginsburg once related her conflicted feelings about resuming work as a lawyer after her first child was born. An early pioneer and one of only a handful of women law students at Harvard in the 1950s, she made her academic mark there after she was appointed to the *Law Review*. For all her recognized outstanding legal abilities, though, Ginsburg had second thoughts about her career path once she started a family. Eventually her father-in-law provided the gentle guidance that helped her decide. He told her that if she gave up law everyone would understand, but if she really wanted to be a lawyer, she would find a way.[1] Ginsburg found a way and went on to become a pivotal figure in the legal battles to secure women's rights. Ultimately she attained the highest legal position in the country.

Almost all mothers consider, at least briefly, whether they can handle both a challenging career and a young family. These thoughts frequently arise in the middle of the night when a mother leaves her bed for the second time to attend to a crying baby or a sick child. Roughly half of women who begin a fast track job will stay the course, but a substantial number, mostly mothers, will drop out or drop down to a less demanding track. Doing so usually isn't really a matter of choice even though some mothers believe it is. Working parents are forced out by backward family leave policies, the escalating demands of the workplace, and a society that increasingly points a finger at mothers' ambitions.

Some women, especially those who are married to affluent partners, find that dropping out of the workplace suits their priorities and ambitions, at least for a time. It affords a chance to focus on parenting when children need the most attention. In this sense, the second tier and a temporary stay-at-home option are welcome alternatives to the rigid 9-to-5 track. But most mothers do not realize that dropping down will close doors permanently, even when a part-time track is advertised as a temporary alternative.

Why some mothers take alternative routes while others stay the course may be the most important story in the life course of professional women.

THE CAREER–FAMILY TRADEOFF: HISTORICAL TRENDS

"Choices" women make today—to have children but stay the course, to drop out or drop down, or to decline motherhood entirely—are not unique to modern women.

Harvard economist Claudia Goldin reminds us that each generation of twentieth-century women perceived this "choice" somewhat differently. In fact, women have followed five distinctly different patterns, each seriously constrained by historical events. The first cohort she tracks includes the relatively few and mostly privileged women who graduated from college between 1900 and 1920, the first generation to receive a higher education in any significant numbers. They decided on either career or family but not both. Many chose careers, largely as teachers, social workers, and librarians. Thirty percent of these women did not marry and 50 percent did not have children.[2] This was the generation that produced suffrage leaders like Alice Paul and social reformers such as Jane Adams.

The next generation, those who graduated from college between 1920 and 1945, chose job first, then family. These jobs were meant to last for a few years, not to become lifetime careers. These women, who experienced the economic devastation of the Great Depression and the turmoil of World War II, were less likely to choose a professional career, a path considered reserved for men, and gave up their jobs when they had children. Only 15 to 20 percent never married and the majority (60–65 percent) had children.[3]

The postwar generation of college graduates (1945–1965) was the most domestic and fertile generation. These women were far more likely than either their mothers or grandmothers had been to marry early and have several children. Only 8 percent remained single and 83 percent had children.[4] Members of this maternal stay-at-home generation, venerated in timeless 1950s TV domestic sitcoms such as *Leave It to Beaver* and *I Love Lucy*, sometimes found a part-time job after the children were grown, but rarely a career. These are the mothers of the pioneers.

The baby boomers, the numerous children of the war generation, are the pioneers of this book. Graduating from college between 1965 and 1985, they chose careers first and then family. This was the generation that opened the doors to careers experienced by only a few of their mothers, grandmothers, or great-grandmothers. They married late and 28 percent never had children.[5]

The last generation examined, those who graduated in the 1980s and 1990s, talked about career and family, and managed to achieve at both slightly better than their mothers had. Only 26 percent are childless at forty.[6] But their story is still unfolding.

EQUALITY INTERRUPTED: FAMILY LEAVE POLICIES

The challenge of gender equality in the workplace asserted by the women's movement was premised on a national commitment to caring for children and an equal partnership at work and at home. This entailed changing not just the rules but also the heart and soul of the culture. Under pressure from NOW (National Organization for Women), Congress passed the Comprehensive Child Development Act of 1971, the first national attempt to provide a general solution for all working mothers. It used a sliding scale communal child care option for all, including middle-class parents. President Nixon, however, vetoed the bill, stating that it undermined the working family.[7] Nixon's concern betrayed his underlying belief that communal child care is connected with communism. This is the kind of thing Russians do, while American families take care of their own children. Nixon's veto terminated the most important effort by the federal government to consider a national policy to accommodate the entrance of mothers into workplace. More than twenty years and many bitter struggles later, a diminished nod to family demands occurred with passage the Family Medical Leave Act of 1993. This welcome but stingy act offers twelve weeks of leave for family medical issues, including childbirth—all unpaid.

Failing to accommodate for paid family leave not only projects a lack of political will but also reflects a persistent cultural reluctance to accept mothers in the workplace. Today, as we shall see, this reluctance manifests itself in a cultural revival of mother shaming, a "new momism" that points a finger at mothers who work, particularly in fast track jobs, while continuing to emphasize the male-only breadwinner role. Still, many mothers persist and thrive.

STAYING THE COURSE

All successful fast track mothers, like Ginsburg, are torn by their competing roles as mother and career woman. The number of mothers who "find a way" of persisting in fast track careers through the make-or-break years and beyond is hard to pin down; many women divert into a less competitive track upon completing their degrees, and few studies follow careers over the life course. But our examination of mothers in the university world and other studies of law and medicine reveal that at least half of mothers who enter the fast track remain through the make-or-break years and beyond. Women who have gone through the grueling training period of a fast track career clearly have an incentive to stay the course—and many do.

Laraine Zappert's survey of Stanford women MBAs from 1975 to the present provides a glimpse into the experience of the fastest track of businesswomen. Stanford MBAs are the young elite groomed for the top corporate positions. For these high fliers sixty-hour weeks and frequent travel are the norm. During the 1970s there were few women in this prestigious graduate program, but female enrollment climbed to nearly 40 percent in the 1990s. Of women who had children (about half), 47 percent worked full-time. About the same number (46 percent) were sidetracked and worked part-time. Only 7 percent labeled themselves as "stay at home," what we now refer to as "opt out" mothers.[8]

The full-time working mothers, many of them on the fastest track, expressed the highest level of contentment. They worked long hours but had little ambivalence. One MBA mother explained, "I feel I have struck the right balance between a fulfilling career and raising my daughters. To me it's been an important legacy for my daughters—to see that my work matters to me and to know what I have been able to accomplish."[9]

Other professions support a higher percentage of mothers who remain on the fast track. In the university world more than half of mothers (55 percent) who have landed tenure track positions go on to receive tenure.[10] In medicine, perhaps unsurprisingly given that there are more tracks, the numbers are even higher. Female doctors are only marginally more likely (5 percent) to leave the profession than male doctors.[11]

Mothers who persist do remarkably well. They don't do as well as men, but they compete favorably with women who don't have children. In universities, mothers are as likely to obtain tenure as other women.[12] In a study of a major financial institution, mothers with children under six earned more and were promoted more quickly than women without children. Authors Mary Blair-Loy and Amy S. Wharton comment, "Mothers maintaining corporate careers are corporate treasures. They work long hours and show high levels of achievement despite their responsibilities at home." Supporting a work–family balance in high finance, it turns out, not only does not jeopardize productivity, it may lead to higher levels of performance over a woman's career. Staying the course pays off for both mothers and corporations.[13]

The most successful mothers take their parental leave following childbirth for a few weeks or a few months and then return as full-time workers. They don't move to a part-time track because it's unavailable or, in many cases, unacceptable—to do so, they believe, would be the kiss of death to their career. A study of University of Michigan Law School graduates found that women who became partners worked less than full-time for one year and spent only 1.7 months out of the labor force.[14] Somehow these mothers overcome the emotional and physical pull of the infant and the forbidding judgment of a society which increasingly sends the message that mothers who can afford to stay home should do so.

The successful mothers we interviewed share many winning characteristics: physical stamina, an ambitious nature, and just plain luck. Rather than cite their own exceptional qualities, these women note that many mothers who opt out are equally talented and capable. They have seen that a sick child, a divorce, a husband's relocation, or any number of unpredictable life events can derail a colleague's career.

Supportive partners and time management skills top their list of explanations for their own success. Our research shows that a small band of single mothers also succeed, usually with a supportive network of family and close friends.[15] All of our successful mothers exhibited the ability to manage the details of everyday work and family life with great efficiency. As one mother said, "I always have sixteen balls in the air at any moment."

MOTHER TIME

Successful mothers get the workplace to work for them. They get their work done, but in a different time frame than men. I think of it as "mother time." Mothers, like male lawyers, put in more than full-time hours, but they leave the office promptly at 5:00. They are not available for late-night or weekend work, and they don't travel if they can help it. Still, they get the work done, and most win a grudging acceptance, not only from their boss but also from coworkers. In the university world, it's the mothers who insist on, and almost always win, the concession that departmental meetings end by 5:00 P.M. Their coworkers have come to accept their schedule and trust that they are shouldering their full load.

Senior partner in a major law firm and mother of two Jessica Pers describes how she has flexibly managed her daunting requirement of billable hours: "When my children were still in high school, I went to every baseball game and I went to every soccer game . . . The billable hours expectation for the year is 2,400 hours but these can be done in any conceivable configuration, whether it means getting to the office at 7:00 A.M. and leaving early or getting there at 9:00, leaving at 4:00, and starting work again at 7:00 and working to midnight." Pers notes that the technology revolution—the arrival of the personal computer, cell phone, and PDA—has increased personal time management and flexibility of schedule. These mobile devices enabled moms like Pers to triage clients from the sidelines of soccer games. "[Clients] don't care where you are as long as you are accessible. You are unfortunately always available, but you are able to work in the intricacies of your life."

An important skill for career mothers to master is the ability to say no. Refusing most evening meetings and travel is a difficult but necessary strategy. For some lucky mothers, the workplace occasionally accommodates their travel needs; my university offers travel allowances which cover the extra expenses that academic mothers with infants incur when attending conferences. But often there is no institutional help, and a mother must find other ways to keep up with her work.

Jessica Pers handled the travel problem differently. At age forty-two, she took over the most prestigious and arguably the most demanding job in her law firm—managing partner—to spend more time at home. "I was the managing partner from '92 to '95, starting when I was forty-two, which is young to be a managing partner. According to the legal press I was the first woman to be the managing partner of a multioffice law firm in the country. That was an important 'first' for me and for the firm. In addition, those three years turned out to be very good for me and my family. I got to stay home and not travel so much when my kids were six and nine. In effect, I had a three-year respite from crazy, unpredictable litigation."

There is some evidence that the time management and multitasking skills which working mothers rely on are enhanced by motherhood. In a recent well-publicized scientific study of mother rats and same-age female rats that were not mothers, Craig Kinsley and his colleagues found that mother rats were significantly better at finding Fruit Loops in a maze than were their childless counterparts.[16] An evolutionary explanation is that mothers (or mother rats) are forced to deal with the new challenges of finding food and feeding their young and themselves. Mothers in the workplace succeed by prioritizing their tasks in a creative manner, perhaps using the coping skills honed by evolution.

PARTNERS

Almost without exception, married mothers credited their partners as key to their success. "I you want a career, don't marry a jerk," a prominent engineer told me. Few achieved the equal sharing of domestic responsibilities hoped for by the feminist revolution, but almost all saw their partners as completely supportive. Ruth Bader Ginsburg's husband, Milton, encouraged her career throughout their relationship and they pursued law careers together with equal zeal.

There are small signs of role reversal on the fast track, particularly among the second generation. Many mothers who persist on the fast track command high salaries, often higher than their partners. Some partners welcome this and gladly cut back on work to spend more time with their children. These fathers must overcome the male breadwinner expectation, which is still firmly in place. Carole C., a young lawyer in a major law firm, describes how she and her husband negotiated a role reversal and its delicate social management: "We both come from traditional families and are both very traditional in the sense that we agreed that one of us should stay home, but neither one of us had strong feelings about who it should be. Then it became clear during the pregnancy that he wasn't enjoying practicing law and he really thought he would enjoy being a stay-at-home dad."

Engineering professor Alice Agogino married a fellow engineering student from graduate school but has shouldered most of the professional responsibilities through the years, while her husband has taken over more of the domestic duties. "My husband has never accepted a paying job. He is the head of a huge nonprofit but he works at home. We share the housework. He does more of the cooking and driving our children to and from school."

While Carole's and Alice's husbands may not be the norm, husbands and dads in general are becoming more amenable to sharing the burden of the second shift at home. Today it's common to see a baby's head peeking out of a Snugli on a young man's chest or a father doing diaper duty at home. According to a recent study by the Family and Work Institute, fathers spend an hour a day more on parenting than they did twenty-five years ago—an increase from 1.7 to 2.7 hours.

What makes these partnerships work for career-minded mothers is not necessarily that the parenting is equally shared (women put in 3.4 hours to men's 2.7 hours per day) but that their partners encourage their careers.

THE NANNY WARS

Ever since attorney Zoe Baird was turned down for a federal judgeship in 1993 because she had not paid social security taxes for her nanny, the topic of nannies has been a minefield for professional women. The national media has glossed over the huge number of low-wage, largely immigrant support staff that supports executives—including janitors, construction workers, drivers, and kitchen help. But nannies, properly paid or not, can excite a media frenzy. This issue touches not so much on our concern for exploitation of illegal immigrants, but on our deep cultural ambivalence about allowing others to care for our children.

In-home care is crucial for parents with long and sometimes unpredictable work schedules. Many professional couples, particularly in law and medicine, are well positioned to afford it. According to the 2000 census, professional mothers who work full-time have the highest household income, since they are most likely to be married to professional men. By contrast, professional men are more likely to have stay-at-home wives and therefore lower house-hold incomes.[17]

Jessica Pers, who had her first child while she was still an associate on the partnership track, feels that outside help was key: "We assumed I would go back to work—it never occurred to either one of us that I wouldn't. My husband is the equivalent wage earner; it's as simple as that. We have full-time help so we could focus on our children and each other when we weren't working, rather than on household chores. Luckily for us, we met a wonderful person who has been part of our family for the past twenty-one years."

MOTHER GUILT

Guilt creeps into the thinking of all fast track mothers at some point. They may miss their child's soccer game or feel out of touch with their children's lives. They may question their path and wonder if their choices will negatively affect their family. Successful mothers recognize that neither parenting nor working will get done perfectly. These are women who are used to being the best at whatever they do, and settling for less than perfection can be a difficult adjustment. As Jessica Pers remarks: "To be successful at family and career you have to come to grips with [the fact] that you are not going to be perfect at doing anything. You are not going to be the best mother—I have never made breakfast for my kids and I have never sewn a Halloween costume or whatever it is that all these other mothers seem to be doing. And I am not the best lawyer at my firm either ... but my life is my whole life. My life is my children and my work and my relationship with my husband, and all of that is fine."

Successful working mothers are likely to take challenges in stride and to see their careers in terms of a lifelong commitment. "It is not a twenty-year problem, it is a five-year problem, and in a twenty-six-year career that is not much," says Jessica of the challenges of juggling young children and the fast track. Indeed, the first year following childbirth is critical. The new mother, like all working mothers, must completely restructure her life. But for career women in the first years of a demanding profession with overtime require-ments, the challenge is doubly daunting. The demands of motherhood will change as the child grows older and perhaps a second child is born. Most find older children, with their expanding worlds of school and friends, less of a time burden. Fathers, teachers, and baby-sitters begin to play a larger caretaking role. If the working mother can make it through the toughest years of raising an infant, she may find balancing career and family becomes easier with time. Women with a long-term perspective on mother guilt are most likely to stay the course.

OPTING OUT

Recently the media has focused rather mean-spirited attention on successful career mothers who "opt out" permanently.[18] The thrust of the argument is that successful professional women married to affluent, successful men choose to abandon their profession to stay home with the children. The implication is that a career is a preference, like maintaining a second home, that has become too hard to manage, and years of training and commitment are easily dispensed with. These reports don't expose the tangle of ambivalence and regret experienced by most women who make this choice—or the fact that some women have no choice.

Mothers who drop out of their profession each have their own story to tell. Many share my experience—they have the drive to succeed but they have an unsupportive partner, a child with special needs, or a parent who needs special care. For others, the desire for a career continues after childbirth, but the demands of the workplace—sixty-hour weeks in law firms for example— make parenting unfeasible. Many consider themselves a failure, as I did when I left the practice of law.

Each mother makes a decision based on her own circumstances, yet there are common factors that greatly influence whether a mother will remain on the fast track. The culture of the workplace is central; some institutions are more welcoming than others. The role of partners, who may not fully support a mother's career, is also critical, and recently the new momism, a renewed cultural emphasis on the critical role of mothers in a child-centered society, has placed additional pressure on working mothers.

Money also plays into the decision to return or not to work, full- or part-time. Few women can afford to opt out entirely. Women in the richest 5 percent of the population are among the few who can afford to stay out of the labor force for an extended period time. But these days most young women bear the burden of their college and professional school debt through-out their early adulthood. In all urban areas the cost of raising children is more than most single salaries can support.[19]

THE NEW MOMISM

Today's opt-out mothers often don't acknowledge the major shift in cultural attitudes that may have affected their decision to stay at home. In spite of the institutional and cultural advances pushed through by the feminists of my generation, young women with professional ambitions today have a more difficult time integrating their career lives with motherhood than did the pioneer generation, making the "choice" even less voluntary. The demands of the workplace have increased, but the demands of motherhood have ex-ploded. Children now require constant attention. In the 1970s, kids were still allowed to play outdoors by themselves; the national milk carton campaign alerting parents to the terrors of child abduction had not yet panicked the nation. Caitlin Flanagan, in her memoir of her mother returning to work, *To Hell with All That,* describes a 1970s childhood that did not require contin-uous adult supervision: "By the time I was five, I was allowed to wander away from the house so long as I didn't cross any big streets; I had the run of the neighborhood at six. So the idea that I would be home alone in the afternoons at the age of twelve was not a radical or an overly worrisome one for my mother."

This style of parenting did not elicit social censure as it sometimes does today: "Such an arrangement was not then seen as a shocking dereliction of duty: a nine-year-old could be trusted with a key; a nine-year-old knew how to work a telephone if anything went wrong."[20]

Children were not yet fully booked with after-school and weekend activ-ities that require a full-time manager and chauffeur. Homework did not begin in preschool or require hours of parental involvement each night.

Susan Douglas and Meredith Michaels in their book, *The Mommy Myth,* entertainingly but correctly observe the contradiction in this new trend: "Central to the new momism, in fact, is the feminist insistence that women have choices, that they are agents in control of their own destiny, that they have autonomy. But there's where the distortion of feminism occurs. The only truly enlightened choice to make as a woman, the one that proves, first, that you are a 'real' woman, and second that you are a decent, worthy one, is to become a 'mom' and to bring to childrearing a combination of selflessness and professionalism that would involve the cross cloning of Mother Teresa with Donna Shalala. Thus the new momism is deeply contrary: it both draws from and repudiates feminism."[21]

The requirements of the new momism have escalated in other ways as well. Ironically, as women have moved into the workplace, breast-feeding has become not just popular but a requirement of good motherhood. My mother's generation of stay-at-home moms didn't breast-feed; formula was considered the healthier, modern choice, and in its own way, a form of quiet liberation. My mother could leave me with her mother while she joined her soldier husband, my father, on furlough from war duty, for a romantic weekend. She was not physically bound to my feeding schedule.

In my generation breast-feeding regained popularity as an option but not a requirement. Today's mothers are strongly pressured to breast-feed for several months, and are subject to social censure if they choose not to do so. Those who work full-time go to extraordinary lengths to pump and preserve. Refrigerators in workplace coffee rooms contain mothers' milk in glass jars, neatly labeled with a name and time of production. For all working mothers, breast-feeding is a challenge; for mothers on the fast track, it can force a decision to leave the high-pressure workplace.

And today's generation no longer has the women's movement to cheer it on. Most young women do not consider themselves part of this movement and know little, if anything, about its historical significance. The women's movement focused on promoting women into male-dominated power structures, emphasizing equal parenting and a movement away from the romanticized motherhood of the nineteenth century.

Like thousands of other young women in the 1970s, I sat on the floor in someone's tiny living room once a week with seven or eight other young women and argued about "a woman's place." Feminist scholars were vigorously tackling the issue of "difference" between men and women. Gender, which covered virtually all differences except for the obvious physical ones, was seen largely as a social construction created to keep women in a subordinate position.

The full-time homemaker, according to some of these critics, was one of the most potent social constructions. It effectively locked women out of male spheres of power and insinuated its way into mothers' thinking by making some believe it was their own choice to remain at home while fathers strode out into the world. And the result, isolated motherhood, was not good for the children. As prominent sociologist Jessie Bernard argues in *The Future of Marriage*, "assigning sole responsibility for child care to the mother— cutting her off from the easy help of others in an isolated household, requiring round-the-clock tender loving care, and making such care her exclusive activity—is not only new and unique, but not a good way for either women or children."[22]

The venerated anthropologist Margaret Mead was also pulled into the debate. She proclaimed that the mother–child bond, as it was being interpreted in American law, was "a subtle form of anti-feminism in which men— under the guise of exalting the importance of maternity—are tying women more tightly to their children than has been thought necessary since the invention of bottle feeding and baby carriages."[23]

As a new mother, I could not really believe that the powerful feelings my little son evoked in me were totally a matter of cultural conditioning, but I could understand how my society—husband, family, friends, and employers— conspired, in a well-meaning way, to keep me at home permanently.

Whatever their reasons, mothers who decide to stay home with children today, as in the pioneer generation, do so with ambivalence. Many see it as a failure, and few do not harbor guilty regrets. Most tell themselves that it's not permanent, that they will get back to their profession at some point in the future when the children are older.

REENTRY

Women who opt out of the workforce in order to have children often express a desire to pick up their career at a later date. While expressing satisfaction with their "choice," most also talk about returning to work someday.

Most of these "opt out" mothers do return to work at some point, but likely in the second tier or in a marginally related field. The freelance or part-time work they pursue is unlikely to allow them to reenter the fast track.

If and when mothers decide to resurrect their careers a few years later, many will face an unwelcoming job market. "It's hard to get back in. You get branded as a mother. To employers, you can either be nurturing or competent. You can't be both," Kristin Maschka, director of Mothers & More, a networking, education, and support group for mothers with chapters nationwide, said in a recent *USA Today* interview.[24]

These are the mothers for whom the fast tracks are least forgiving. Reentry programs are virtually unheard-of in these professions, and there is little support from professional organizations, women's organizations, or families. The statistics portray the harsh reality of reentry. Although 93 percent of highly qualified women want to return to work after taking time off, only 40 percent successfully return to full-time jobs.[25] And on average, these women lost 18 percent of their earning power when they returned to work after taking a break.[26]

WORKPLACE PRESSURES

The workplace environment is critical in determining whether a young mother can make her new life work. CBS executive Missy Rennie recalls the atmosphere when she had her first child. "The decision to have children complicated my pure love of my work. When I had my first child at CBS, I was one of the only pregnant women walking the halls; it was not part of the culture of the place. By the time I had my second child in 1987 that had changed; there were many more pregnant women and allowances for family needs."

Ten years after Rennie had her first child, the president of CBS had a child and became much more receptive to the needs of working mothers. But the first career women who had families opened the doors for both sexes, believes Rennie. "It made women feel more comfortable verbally asserting their needs, [such as wanting] to go to the school plays. When I got to CBS news, hostages were being held in Tehran and it was not clear if the producer who was in Tehran would be allowed to leave to attend his own wedding. That discussion just would not happen today; there's a sense that people have to have a personal existence put into the equation. It's women who completely changed these work environments."

The density of mothers influences the cultural climate of the workplace. While one rarely sees children in biology laboratories, large law firms, or even hospitals, in workplaces where there are more mothers there is usually more flexibility.

Some women believe that they're better off keeping their family obligations out of the workplace and may not mention their children at work. "I had a very difficult time when my children were young," said Paula, a senior partner in a large accounting firm. "But I kept my work life and home life separate, and I think that's the way it should be. Women don't do themselves any favors when they ask for special privileges; it only hurts their careers, and makes it hard for other women."

The American workplace is largely unprepared to accommodate new mothers. Parental leaves of twelve weeks are now federally mandated under the Family Medical Leave Act, but there is no mandate to pay the employee for that time. Many of the fast track professions do offer fully or largely paid parental leaves—some as long as six months. As with most family-friendly policies, large corporations have taken the lead, goaded by the decades-long political campaign to secure family medical leave policies. They are a welcome change, and most new mothers take advantage of them. Many, however, fear that an extended leave will seriously hurt their chances for promotion. Fathers rarely take full advantage of parental policies.

Many colleges and universities offer to stop the clock on the tenure race for up to one year to accommodate the needs of new parents. Some also offer up to six months of reduced or even waived professional obligations—effectively a six-month maternity leave. These family-friendly options are offered to both fathers (who claim to be the primary caretaker) and mothers who, by definition, are considered to be so. Mothers are often afraid to take advantage of these policies.

One assistant professor mother said, "I know that when it comes time for tenure they will just count my publications and divide by the years—they won't care about the year when they are supposed to stop the clock. And they will notice that I taught less than others. I just can't take that chance."[27]

Fathers don't often use these accommodations for parents, even when they are full participants in parenting because, like mothers, they fear they'll be considered less committed to their career, which may diminish their chances at tenure. Not surprisingly, women who already have tenure (a much smaller number) are far more likely to take advantage of these important benefits.[28]

There are signs that the corporate world is moving to become more accommodating to mothers. In June 2004 Deloitte & Touche announced that it would allow employees to leave the company for up to five years to attend to family obligations. Participants in the program are considered "alumni" who will return to the company in the near future. Deloitte & Touche provides resources to help alumni keep their job skills current and stay connected to the firm.[29]

But the parental leave is the easy part; the hard part is returning to a demanding, unchanged workplace after a life-changing event like having a child. The new mother cannot, on the spur of the moment, stay late to meet a critical deadline or take a client to dinner. Nor does she want to. She is pulled, as if by a powerful magnet, to attend to the needs of her newborn. The needs of an infant trump the pressure to attend a conference or business meeting or to hold a face-to-face meeting with a client.

But mothers don't all feel this way. Some women feel comfortable leaving their infant in the hands of a caretaker and return to work eagerly.

Zoologist Sarah Hrdy, in her insightful book *Mother Nature,* reminds us that many of the same hormones stimulated in childbirth and breast-feeding occur during sexual attraction; it's an important biological mechanism for guaranteeing the protection of the young of many species.[30] The pull that young mothers feel is to a certain extent built into our biological makeup. Workplace pressures are not just external to mothers; often they are internal too.

But Hrdy also points out that humans cannot be raised by a mother alone. The species requires several individuals, whom she terms "alloparents" to assist in raising a child. "In many species of birds, and in about 10% of mammals, including a tiny fraction of primates (humans and a few species of monkeys and prosimians that bear multiple young), infant survival depends upon the mother being assisted by mothers—the father and/or various individuals other than the parents—alloparents."[31] With few exceptions, human beings have been raised throughout their history in large family units, with many supporting adults.

MOONLIGHTING

There are other reasons why mothers, after a great deal of soul searching, leave the fast track. The "second shift" can break a mother's back. Even if she has a support system in place, the hours at work combined with the hours at home take their toll. Our study of nine thousand faculty in the University of California system, which measured professional, housework, and caregiving time, indicated that mothers with children in the household report working ninety-four hours a week, twenty-seven on caregiving, while fathers work eighty-two hours per week; twenty hours on caregiving. Men and women without children clock in at seventy-seven hours of work in total. The energy and stamina that have carried these mothers through years of intensive academic and professional training may not be enough to take on the double load. Physical stamina cannot be underestimated as a factor in career success, particularly for mothers.[32]

The demands of the workplace are hard enough for working mothers, but when the second shift at home is heaped on top of them, women face a schedule that's unsustainable. In a study of women with at least one child who had occupied high-level positions in the corporate world for an average of thirteen years, workplace conditions were cited as the number one reason why mothers leave jobs to return home. The survey by Pamela Stone and Meg Lovejoy showed that a large part of this discontent focused on the new breakneck pace of the workplace and company mergers. "The high-tech workweek is really sixty hours, not forty. Nobody works 9 to 5 anymore,"

Everybody Is Very Busy

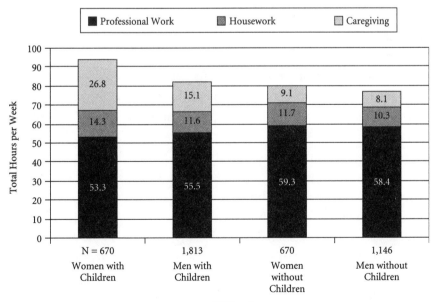

Source: Mary Ann Mason, Angelica Stacy, and Marc Goulden, The UC Faculty Work and Family Survey, 2003 (http://ucfamilyedge.berkeley.edu).

notes one respondent.[33] When companies merge, as they increasingly do, any sense of a "family" environment disappears.

But these mothers did not leave their positions so easily. About 90 percent of the mothers expressed a moderate to high degree of ambivalence about their decision and for many, it was an agonizing choice. A senior editor at a publishing house said, "My whole identity was work. Yes, I was a mother and a wife and whatever, but this is who I was."[34]

DROPPING DOWN: THE "MOMMY TRACK" AND OTHER SECOND TIER POSITIONS

In the Stanford Business School study nearly half of the mothers moved to a slower track in their corporation or became freelance consultants working from their homes.

Strikingly, many, if not most, of the part-time and stay-at-home moms in the study did not consider their current career choice to be a permanent arrangement. They anticipated returning to the full-time workforce after their children were launched and on the school track. However, as the author admits, "Because very few women with grown children had themselves experimented with sequencing, we have little data on how well this plan works over time."[35]

Some lucky mothers may have the opportunity to switch to a viable part-time track with rights of return to full-time within the same workplace. But most part-time tracks are permanent sidetracks. For some women, this track is a welcome escape from the rat race while for others, it's an inescapable, permanent limbo.

Whether the second tier addresses the needs of working mothers or exploits the arrival of lower paid, highly educated mothers in the labor market is a matter of some debate. What is clear is that the second tier, in all of its manifestations, is the fastest growing sector of medicine, law, and academe. It is a topic that will be considered profession by profession in the next chapter.

5

The Second Tier

The majority of part-timers are women who stay at 40 percent time (for the benefits). For these lifers it's always a struggle and always a battle...it is very clear to many of us as part-time people in the academic system that it is not a good route to a tenure track position: they hire out.
—Leslie Z., university lecturer

I'm able to work when my kids are sleeping and if they're making noise or watching *Barney* nobody knows it since I work online...I thought I would go back to a traditional job working as an engineer, but I just never felt that way.
—Cheryl Demas, entrepreneur and work-at-home mom

Annalee Rejohn has been a part-time lecturer in Celtic studies and comparative literature at UC Berkeley for nearly thirty years. She began at Berkeley as a teaching assistant and married a professor. They had a child after she completed her first book, and she opted to take a job that would give her the flexibility to raise a family and accommodate her husband's career. "It was really rough at first. There was no security. I didn't know from one term to the other whether I would have a job," she says. When lecturers at the university unionized, they saw improved job security in the form of three-year contracts, but the pay and benefits remain poor. Annalee continues to teach and publish but her career is on hold. "I have kept up my scholarship—I have published and organized conferences, and I am now writing my third book—but I get no credit for that as a lecturer. Fortunately my husband has family health benefits, which adequately cover our family."

Dr. P., an internist, has two young school-age children and works four days a week in a group practice. "This suits me," she says. "I can increase my hours when I want to, or cut back—there are other doctors to cover for me. I am only on call one weekend a month." Since having children, she no longer teaches at the medical school or accepts interns for training. "My schedule now does not make training possible; they need more attention than I can give them." Dr. P. had originally planned to be a neurologist, but her lack of aptitude for the subject and a desire to have an easier schedule led her to choose internal medicine.

Cheryl Demas, a mother of two and a former engineer with a private firm, decided to get off the corporate track and start her own business. She gave up her full-time job to have more time for her kids and now runs a small publishing operation out of her home.

Cheryl Demas, Dr. P, and Annalee Rejohn are all mothers working in the "second tier" of their profession. Dr. P. may increase her hours, but she is not going to become the chief of staff or the dean of a medical school. Annalee may continue to publish in distinguished journals and may win awards in her field, but she is unlikely to become a professor at a major university. Cheryl may excel at her own business, but she is not on track to become a major executive at a Fortune 500 company. However, all three women will be actively engaged in their children's lives while maintaining a professional identity.

Their stories reflect the growing bifurcation of all fast track careers: a first tier of prestigious, well-paid jobs dominated by men and an expanding second tier composed largely of women with children. Across the professions, this second tier, whether full-time or part-time, is a less demanding, slower track. Sometimes it has lower status and pays less with little chance for advancement. The second tier is controversial; it's both lamented and celebrated by the women working in it.

My own experience in the second tier, first as a part-time lecturer and then as a full-time midlevel manager at a small college, probably mirrors the ambivalence of many women caught in this career limbo. I was in these positions because I couldn't manage a high-pressure law career and a family at the same time. I needed the money and I enjoyed my work—it was a welcome break from raising young children—and I had stimulating students and pleasant colleagues in both positions. I was able to pick up my children by 5:00 and have dinner on the table by 6:00. I didn't think too far into the future—small children have a way of pinning you to the present. But as they grew more independent, I became restless. I wrote a book, mostly out of passion for the topic and for the writing experience, but in the back of my mind I hoped it would give me a second chance at a new career—and it did. For most women, though, the door does not open again.

This new stratum of high-profile professions has evolved with the dramatic cultural and labor force shifts of the past quarter of a century. It's well-known that predominantly female professions, like grammar and high school teaching, nursing, and social work, offer less pay and lower status than male-dominated professions, such as law, medical practice, and corporate management. But we are now seeing the second tier emerge in previously male-dominated professions with a new, nearly equal gender distribution. A closer look reveals differences within these seemingly gender-balanced professions: women are segregated in a reduced-hour, underpaid second tier.

Without much note, these structural shifts are remaking the professions. In higher education, the tipping point occurred around the millennium when, for the first time, the U.S. Department of Education reported that part-time faculty or adjuncts taught 40 percent of all college courses.[1] At about the same time, law firms began to consolidate into practices of one hundred partners or more, and HMOs began to attract solo physicians into salaried positions.[2] The old model of high-status professions—a small shop of skilled professionals with a limited support staff—is gradually but relentlessly being replaced by a corporate model. The new structure is pyramidal with a small number of executives dictating to a large middle management, which prevails over an even larger body of support workers, many of whom are working at sharply reduced rates.

Law firms, corporations, medicine, and the university world largely perceive the second tier as an opportunity to use skilled labor at a discount price. Or at least this is the uncritical manner in which the second tier has evolved.

The growth of the second tier is also closely tied to the demands of the fast track. Men and women who persist in the fast track are perceived by their employers as "ideal workers."[3] Work is their primary focus, and all other personal pursuits, including family, take a backseat. Many new mothers (and some new fathers), while dedicated to the professions they have spent years preparing for, cannot continue as unqualified "ideal workers," even if they remain deeply committed to their profession. They can't put in the extra hours, meet the around-the-clock deadlines, and travel across the continent for face-to-face negotiations when asked. For them, leaving the fast track isn't always a considered, conscious decision. They are not offered an alternative way of remaining on the fast track in a lower gear for any period of time.

In this sense the second tier is a practical solution to the thorny problem of work–family balance. Mothers like Dr. P. find the hours and flexibility of the slower track crucial to continuing to practice their profession. Many professionals, both men and women, are not interested in the frantic pace that usually characterizes rising to the top of the profession. The second tier is a welcome exit off this unsustainable track and lifestyle. For some women it represents an ideal compromise: it allows them to remain involved in professional life while escaping the stress of balancing upward mobility against the demands of family life. Some mothers take advantage of their skills and their relative freedom to create new businesses, start new nonprofits, or write the books they could not undertake as media executives.

Yet others, like Annalee Rejohn, the part-time lecturer at UC Berkeley, believe it's an unfair system that permanently marginalizes workers who often put in the same hours and produce a similar scholarly output as most full-time professors. Many women will argue that their priorities shift after they start a family. Certainly the imperative of small children requires a new focus. But as Jessica Pers, the attorney introduced in the previous chapter, notes, the matter of choice clearly arises when a mother is ready and eager to return to her profession. And some who "choose" the second tier do not always realize that there is rarely a way back to the fast track. In most cases, mothers eager to return to their profession are welcomed only into the second tier, if at all. Women see this as a personal failure and not as a structural barrier.

The second tier should not have to be a frustrating compromise, a bitter resolution to thwarted ambitions. And barring women from the first tier, a trend that could emerge from the growing bifurcation of the professions, should not be allowed. In order for women to have a true choice in their career trajectory, the second tier should be elective and should include opportunities to return to the fast track.

MEDICINE: THE COMFORTABLE SECOND TIER

Second tier options have been most successfully implemented in medicine. Indeed, medicine offers a promising and evolving model of the feminization of a male-dominated, high-status profession. Many factors—most acutely the runaway inflation of medical costs over the past twenty years—have forced the reinvention of the medical delivery model. Medicine, even more than other male-dominated professions, has grown increasingly corporate, with large group practices and institutionalized health systems taking over small private practices. In part this evolution can occur because there is a swelling labor force of women physicians willing to work within the new model. While some doctors looking for greater balance in their lives welcome this kind of work, experts say that it has created an increasing pink-collar level of medicine in which more women are concentrated in the lowest-paying, least prestigious specialties.

Indeed, while the number of women practicing medicine has more than tripled in the past twenty years, female doctors still earn roughly two-thirds of their male counterparts' salaries, largely because they work fewer hours and because there are fewer of them in the most prestigious and highest-paid specialties. Of all residents studying surgical specialties in 1997, only 17.2 percent were women.[4]

Overall, doctors' net earnings are lower than in the past, but the losses are concentrated in primary care, where most women practice. Women currently represent 52 percent of family practice residents and 74.5 percent of obstetrics and gynecology residents, while men represent 73.3 percent of general surgery residents.[5] Women residents also are well represented in internal medicine (42 percent), pediatrics (69 percent), and dermatology (60 percent).[6]

But this gap is generational as well as gender related. Income has declined for male doctors under fifty as more physicians—male and female—are pushed by the HMO model toward primary care.[7] Women without children are moving toward the same income levels as men, and both men and women are putting in fewer hours than a decade ago. Women with children are falling behind those without children but are putting in even fewer hours. Overall, female primary care physicians report lower annual income (60 percent to 85 percent of male primary care physicians) and lower income per hours worked (between 71 percent and 98 percent of those of their male counterparts).[8]

The good news is that women physicians are more likely to have children and less likely to divorce than other fast track professionals, and they are unlikely to drop out of their profession. Fewer than 10 percent of women leave the medical profession.[9] Overall, the move toward managed care is transforming physicians into salaried employees who put in their shift and go home. Most women doctors still put in relatively long hours, but their workweek, particularly in HMO settings and large practices, may be forty hours rather than the sixty hours routinely clocked in by other physicians. Part-time and "flex" options are disproportionately used by female doctors. A recent survey by the Commonwealth Fund found that 25 percent of female doctors reported working fewer than forty hours a week, compared with 12 percent of male doctors.[10] That trend is most pronounced among younger doctors; on average female doctors work 9 percent fewer hours than male doctors, but among those under forty-five, the number surges to 15 percent.[11]

In addition to more reasonable work schedules, medicine offers women several other advantages. A medical degree holds its market value (even if the recipient drops out for a number of years) to a degree that other professional degrees do not. A seven-year-old law degree or Ph.D. without continuous service will not impress many employers. A medical degree with a seven-year employment gap will still open doors to jobs.

Women physicians, for whatever reason, are likely to be married to other physicians. This fact does not foster greater equity in parenting, but it does generate higher household income. According to the 2000 census, married women physicians report the highest household income of all the professions.[12] More money allows for more household help; this may help explain the low dropout rate of women physicians.

The second tier of medicine does not offer the most power, the highest wages, or the highest status, but it is a comfortable tier where dedicated women can still become mothers and fully engage in their profession with the expectation of a reasonable income and stature in the community. They may not reach the "first tier" of medicine—the prestigious surgical specialties and the top ranks of academic medicine and administration, which are still dominated by men—but many second tier doctors don't particularly want to. This gender division in medical practice is creating an increasingly bifurcated profession.

Landing in the second tier isn't always a matter of conscious choice because mothers often have few alternatives. Panna Losey, a family care practitioner and part-time hourly wageworker in Santa Rosa, California, has spent most of her working life in the second tier of modern medical practice. After college Panna entered the Peace Corps and began medical school upon her return. After watching several friends grapple with parenting during medical training, she decided that path was unsustainable. "In the residency program a good friend had two children and it was brutal. Her kids were angry at her and she was tired at work—she could do neither well. During residency it takes all of your daylight hours—you hardly get to see young kids." Between the demands of work and family, Panna realized that finding time for anything else would be difficult. Like many younger doctors, she didn't want her job to consume her life. "Most choices I made about my career, in terms of part-time and being a family doctor, had less to do with family and more to do with having a life outside of work. I want to do other things with my life," she said.

THE 9-TO-5 SPECIALTIES

There are other options for women in medicine beyond primary care. Some high-prestige specialties (for example, dermatology, anesthesiology, radiology, and emergency room medicine) offer reasonable hours and represent viable alternatives for physician mothers. While residency and additional training add on years at the front end, flexibility is possible once the specialty degree is in hand, and the pay is greater than in primary care. Another advantage of emergency medicine and anesthesiology is that the hospital is the employer and the physician receives a check without having to deal with insurance companies.

Emergency room medicine, historically a catchall position that includes employed doctors with various training backgrounds, has become a focused specialty with rigorous training. Its attractions include the heart-catching dramas captured on the television program *ER,* but also the freedom to release patients to other doctors without the responsibility of follow-up. When a shift is over, the doctor, who may have treated a dozen patients, is no longer responsible for any of them. He or she will not receive a call in the middle of the night from an acutely ill patient. ER medicine is high stress and high burnout, making it perhaps less attractive than dermatology for a parent hoping to juggle work and family. This is still largely a man's field, with only 28 percent of current female residents, but their numbers are growing.

Barb B. is part of that 28 percent minority. A mother and an ER doctor, she's made key sacrifices to reconcile her demanding profession with her family life. Barb began her career as a biological researcher but was just as focused on playing rugby and eventually became a member of the U.S.

national rugby team. While in her thirties she took stock of her priorities and decided to switch careers and pursue a medical degree. "I remember distinctly seeing a photograph in the *New York Times* of a lesbian couple who were both doctors, and I thought: I could do this."

While studying at Berkeley, Barb met her partner, Karie, a Ph.D. student. They exchanged vows in 2000 while Barb was still in medical school and had a daughter in 2001. When the time came to choose a specialty, Barb picked emergency medicine with the idea that it would afford more flexibility. "I wanted a program that was family friendly where other people had children, but I did not want to ask too much at the residencies; I did not want to put everything on the table. Your job is to go and work and put in your hours and focus on work, not family—that is clear. Some programs you could tell it just wouldn't work. In emergency medicine there are three-year and four-year programs and again the four years, the extra year [with shorter shifts] would ideally make more time [for family]."

Ultimately Barb chose a teaching hospital in Oakland, California, where many faculty members have children and she is able to work from 7:00 A.M. to 5:00 P.M. most days with longer shifts when she's on call. Still Barb finds the schedule has taken a toll on her family life. "I have not had a whole weekend off since Christmas; there is no way to make family plans. The program has to come first," she relates. The recently imposed work restrictions (thirty-hour shifts) have been a big help, says Barb, but she still puts in 100 to 120 hours a week relatively often. "Having a child in residency is very difficult; the resident cannot be responsible for the child care at all. Most residents I know with children have a family member in the area. Sometimes I can't do anything [for the family]—pick [my daughter] up or even walk the dog . . . I am lucky to get an hour to play with her before she goes to bed."

While Barb and Karie hope to become equal parents and equal partners in the career world, the truth is that Karie, a Ph.D. in social welfare, has side-lined her career to play the primary parent. They hope that will change. "The schedule [after residency] is always variable but you can work three or four eight-hour shifts a week, and you can take the extra time to be with family, do research, or explore other interests."

For Barb, one thing is clear: her career decisions will be guided, every step of the way, by her drive to find a work–family balance. She believes that emergency medicine, which is demanding but offers flexible shift work, will eventually allow that lifestyle. Her job won't have the status of a surgical or academic position, however, and on some days Barb still entertains the idea of becoming a professor of medicine.

EXITING THE CORPORATE TRACK

Cheryl Demas, a mother of two and engineer who formerly worked with a large company, decided to get off the corporate track in 1994 when her seven-year-old daughter was diagnosed with diabetes. Recognizing that her children would require more attention, she gave up her full-time job and started taking occasional website design work. In 1995 she launched an online magazine for work-at-home moms, which has since become her full-time business. Each year, traffic to her site doubles, and now WAHM.com gets 15,000 to 20,000 hits each day. "I'm able to work when my kids are sleeping. And if they're making noise or watching *Barney*, nobody knows it since I work online," she said. "I thought I would go back to a traditional job working as an engineer, but I just never felt that way," she said.

Women in business are more likely than men to leave the larger corporate world to start or join a new business. This can be anything from a bookstore, software company, or new line of clothing products. The vast majority are small businesses; the Women's Leadership Exchange reports that of the 10.6 million businesses owned by women, only 279,000 gross more than $1 million a year.[13] Over the past two decades women-owned businesses in the United States have taken off. According to the Center for Women's Business Research, as of 2002 there were 6.2 million privately held, majority women-owned businesses employing 9.2 million workers and generating $1.5 trillion in sales.[14]

Women leave traditional corporate jobs for many reasons—to escape middle management limbo with no prospects for advancement, to avoid a hostile or uncaring boss or workplace, and most prominently, to accommodate family responsibilities. A Catalyst student of women entrepreneurs found that, not surprisingly, 82 percent of the women surveyed had children.[15]

Angela, a thirty-four-year-old health care analyst and mother of two, found that after her second child was born, work began to exact more personal sacrifice. "At this point in my life, my career is important, but my kids are *extremely* important to me," she says. "They're getting older so quickly."

Angela's employer, a biotechnology firm, initially refused her request for reduced hours, but when she informed her manager that absent a compromise she would quit, her employer relented. "If there was no bend, it just wouldn't have worked."[16]

"Please don't recount this vote," said former vice president Al Gore at the annual Webby Awards, as he received a lifetime achievement award for Web creation. Recipients are limited to five-word acceptance speeches. This annual event has grown from a raucous party in its San Francisco days to a New York venue with five hundred guests.[17] It is the creation of Tiffany Shlain, a designer for a print magazine, *The Web*, who created the Webby Awards largely as a project she could do from home while managing her newborn.

Shlain, thirty-six, sings the praises of the entrepreneurial world for mothers and points out the advantages the Web offers women and men who work from home. Shlain launched the Webbies while working from home and managing her newborn. Almost all of the work she does in organizing what has become a prominent international media event can be done within hearing distance of her eighteen-month-old daughter. "Since my daughter was born, I have kept a schedule and also try to change it every week. I get time to run errands, to take my daughter to the doctor, to have time with the girls. The Web allows me to be very efficient with my time." Like many work-from-home moms, Tiffany sometimes finds it difficult to "unplug" from the office and the communications technology that keeps her connected to her work. "On Saturdays my husband and I take what we call a 'technology Shabbat' and do not use cell phones, computers, or anything. We have to impose limits on ourselves with all the technology we have in the house."

But Tiffany's success and busy lifestyle would not be possible without these enabling tools. She is currently writing a book about how the Web can allow women to create the schedule they want, especially within more offbeat professions. "Even the waitress mom can use the Internet to study for a new degree, register to vote, and do a variety of tasks that were not possible before the convenience of the Web."

The Internet does offer creative entrepreneurial opportunities and greater flexibility. But for many mothers it can lead to marginalized piecework. Some corporations, especially ones that focus on publishing and technical support, do not require personal client contact or direct collaboration with other workers. They have found that contracting for in-home services cuts their overhead and can increase their productivity. Many overqualified professional women find themselves editing manuscripts or providing quantitative analyses on a piece of a project in total isolation from any other workers. Few of these jobs offer health benefits.

Even Tiffany recognizes that her path has drawbacks. Having a second child will be a challenge because she doesn't have traditional maternity leave benefits and she wonders if she can keep up the pace if she decides to conceive again. "There are projects I want to start but I don't know how they will fare with having morning sickness, say. It is hard—you make your own schedule, which is great, but there is no maternity leave per se. It takes a lot of self-discipline. I push myself very hard but I am looking for an external scheduler."

Melinda, a writer and work-at-home mom based in Seattle, echoes Tiffany's sentiments. After many years working for high-profile magazines and newspapers, in 2001 Melinda decided to opt out and try her luck as a freelance writer. In between answering calls from her book agent and magazine editors, Melinda tends to her active seven-month-old daughter. "The minute I get to work, she seems to need attention," she explains. "I found it was impossible to do the things I used to do because it's so unpredictable when she will be sleeping."

Melinda worried that her editors would give her less work if they knew she was about to have a child and that she would be unable to meet deadlines once the baby was born. "I wasn't sure I should tell my [book] editor that I was pregnant. I was on track to publish a book a year and I didn't want them to think I wasn't serious about all that," she said. "But realistically, I couldn't do that anyway with a small child. Maybe I'll publish a book every two years now, and that's okay with me."

Melinda says she's noticed friends and acquaintances deciding to give up careers all together after their babies are born and she finds the trend troubling. "I worry that people will start to think twice about offering women slots at elite graduate schools because they might think the degree will be wasted on them if they just drop out after having a child." Still, she believes most women who take time off to raise kids aren't opting out for good. "I really hope all of these smart women find their way back to doing productive things," she said. "At some point, maybe ten or more years later, they will all demand their rightful place back in the workplace."

MIDDLE MANAGEMENT LIMBO

In the corporate world women are not as likely to fall off the corporate track, start new businesses, or become consultants as they are to get stuck in middle management. Regardless of their functional and industry distributions, a general trend is affecting U.S. women managers: they are plateauing at midlevel management positions.[18] More than a generation after women began flooding into the labor market, most Fortune 500s don't have a single woman in corporate officer positions; only seven Fortune 500 CEOs are female.[19] According to a recent census, women corporate officers hold only 3.8 percent of the positions that yield the greatest influence and authority in corporations: chairman, CEO, vice chairman, president, COO (chief operating officer), SEVP (senior executive vice president), and EVP (executive vice president).[20] This is at a time when women make up half the labor force in middle management.

"Women are in the wrong place, in the wrong jobs," says Catalyst President Sheila Wellington. Of the women at the top, only 27.5 percent are in-line jobs—positions that have responsibility for profit and loss. The rest of female corporate officers are in staff roles, such as human resources and public relations.[21] While those positions are important, they don't make or break the bottom line and rarely, if ever, lead to the top job.

By definition, middle managers are those who implement strategies and policies, whereas upper-level managers develop them. The numbers indicate that while women have entered the workforce and managerial-level jobs, they are encountering barriers to advancement to positions that would allow them to define organizational strategy and policy. Sales, in particular, and financial management are the best routes to cracking the glass ceiling into top management. Salesmen become sales managers and may be given ever-increasing responsibility for supervising ever-larger units that determine the profit or loss of a corporation. Men dominate line management jobs while women cluster in personnel and public relations. Human resource managers and the public relations staff share a flat career track—their units will never make or break a company, and their level of responsibility is unlikely to increase.

Why are women not in the line management jobs that lead to upper management and CEO? This question was addressed recently when I spoke to a group of women engineers, mostly graduate students and faculty, at the University of Texas. "There is no place to pump your breasts in an airport," complained one woman engineer who had worked in the industry for ten years as a sales manager for a major industrial firm. Her job kept her on the road (or more accurately, in the air) about half of the time. "There is a place to change babies, usually, but not privacy for pumping. The pay is very good and I was on a fast track, lots of promotions, but I couldn't bear the travel after my son was born." On Friday night in any major airport across the country, one can see armies of suited men—and a few women—returning home for the weekend.

On the positive side, corporate jobs in the middle management limbo of human resources or public relations do offer decent pay and benefits and, especially with larger corporations, family-friendly policies that can include part-time possibilities and occasionally on-site day care. Security and pension benefits are not guaranteed as in the past, but the larger the corporation, the more stable the employment.

LAWYERING IN THE SECOND TIER

What happens to women lawyers with children when they fall off the partnership track? Many will go to smaller firms or begin their own practice, but some will leave private practice (i.e., law firms) entirely. Women give up on private practice at a higher rate than men. A recent study tracked the fifteen-year careers of University of Michigan Law School graduates between 1972 and 1985.[22] Women were slightly less likely than men to have begun their careers in private practice (81 percent versus 87 percent), but they were far less likely than men to make partner (39 percent versus 66 percent). Women who do make partner are less likely to be married or have children, and they earn about 80 percent of what male partners do. Most telling, four years out of law school only 67 percent of women were still in private practice of any kind (not necessarily a large firm), as opposed to 79 percent of men. Fifteen years after graduation, only 35 percent of women remained in private practice compared with 57 percent men.[23]

What about the 65 percent of women who have left private practice after fifteen years? This study did not track them, but other studies indicate women who leave the fast track have probably fallen into second tier positions—jobs that may or may not be directly related to law but offer more manageable hours.[24]

As law firms balloon from handfuls of partners to hundreds, the firm structure is evolving into a new hierarchy. At the top are equity or shareholding partners, on the lower rungs are lawyers on contract, often called "of counsel" attorneys, and on the very bottom are the part-timers. The two bottom layers are far more likely to consist of women, usually with children. Other second tier options available to mothers include corporate counsels, government jobs, and nonprofits. Some of these offer fulfilling careers; they all offer better control of time, less pay, and generally lower status.

Maintaining an alternative track is a conscious decision that a firm makes in response to these work–family conflicts. Recouping the high cost of recruiting and training associates who leave in the first few years is impossible. And those who leave may be among the best and brightest. For this reason, most firms have part-time tracks in place, and many are experimenting with other forms of partnership that are less demanding but do not confer shareholder or equity status.[25]

These "sidetracks" from the fast track have proven largely disappointing. Most attorneys believe that choosing to go part-time is tantamount to choosing career forfeiture and that firms, in the end, are not committed to offering part-timers opportunity for career advancement.[26] Ninety-five percent of law firms offer part-time employment but only 3.5 percent of lawyers take advantage of it. Out of that small percentage, 4.8 percent are associates while 2.8 percent are partners. Some studies have observed that lawyers who use part-time programs feel stigmatized, and that full-time attorneys would rather leave their firms than reduce their schedules because of this perception that part-time programs are not effective.[27] One national study indicates that men rarely go part-time, and of the lawyers who do take advantage of part-time lawyering, the majority, if not all, are probably young mothers.[28]

An American Bar Association study, *Balanced Lives*, reports that these problems are compounded by gender bias. Women associates choose to go part-time primarily for family reasons. Therefore, "when lawyers assume that a working mother is unlikely to be fully committed to her career, they more easily remember the times when she left early than the times when she stayed late."[29] This contributes to a lack of desire to mentor these women. Part-time and family responsibilities may, in turn, contribute to the "non-mom resentment" problem. Women without families often have difficulty finding time for relationships that might lead to them. And unmarried associates believed they ended up with disproportionate work because they did not have an acceptable reason for refusing it.[30]

Jessica Pers, a managing partner at a large San Francisco law firm who is centrally involved with promotion decisions within her firm, agrees with this assessment. She assures me that the decision to have children does not incur any negative evaluation for female associates. However, if the mother returns part-time after the child is born, her trajectory will slow and possibly stagnate. There is a pool of part-time lawyers at her firm made up of women and individuals with health concerns or other time-limiting circumstances. This part-time option, special counsel, is far from desirable in her opinion. "It is a very unsatisfied group holding a low status in the firm and with a confused presentation to the world. They do not have the perks of being a shareholder, but they do not have the anxieties either. It is not a situation which the firm promotes—it is a sidetrack from the fast track and one which is a compromise rather than a viable alternative to the full time."

Carole C., a young lawyer at the same firm, echoes the fear of marginalization that reputedly occurs with part-time work. "We (my lawyer husband and I) briefly considered going part-time. However, I think it is sometimes difficult to be a part-time lawyer because your client expects you to be there and the partners expect you to be there, so it can be hard to maintain those boundaries. There is also a common perception that you get less interesting work if you are part-time."

There are other sidetrack options that cater to the needs of parents. Attorneys who do not make partner are sometimes classified indefinitely as second tier attorneys. Over the past two decades, more firms are recognizing the inefficiencies of the up-or-out process and are experimenting with new positions for lawyers short of full equity partnership.[31] These new positions include senior associate, of counsel, and nonequity partner. The key difference between these alternatives and partnership positions is that these employees are contract workers, not owners. Many attorneys argue that these nonpartnership positions and titles such as nonequity partner are just window dressing for second-class status. They may never see the high-profile clients or be invited to exclusive social events.

A National Law Journal survey reveals that a disproportionate number of women fill the ranks of nonequity partners, a second tier partnership that provides the "partner" title and a higher salary than an associate, but not ownership status with a guaranteed cut of the firm's profits. Of the eighty-two firms that supplied data to the study, only 54 percent of women partners had equity, compared with 74 percent of men.[32] Equity partnership represents far more than a title. When an associate is promoted to partner, compensation has nothing to do with the marketplace; it depends on the profitability of the firm and the partner's stake in the company. Nonequity partnership varies among firms, but it is most often viewed in the same way as an advanced associate, with compensation based on hours worked.

While some women attorneys see this as second-class citizenship, others welcome the second tier partnership as a chance to manage pressures and responsibilities. The biggest criticism from women is that a nonequity partnership, like a part-time position, is a dead-end path. They will never have the opportunity to be major players again.[33]

Why do these alternative tracks, "mommy tracks" as they are frequently referred to, fail to provide the desired choice fervently promoted by the pioneer generation? In part because they are not well supported. In one study, 61 percent of all respondents who worked part-time reported that their firm did little or nothing to develop their part-time work arrangement.[34] They also reported that they were usually excluded from decision-making committees and social events. Not everyone rates the "sidetrack" experience negatively, but the overwhelming number of respondents believed that part-time work isn't yet a desirable career option and that transformation of the workplace is still a distant goal.[35]

PRACTICING LAW OUTSIDE THE FIRM

Increasingly, options beyond employment with a large law firm are dwindling. There is an enormous gulf in prestige, income, and the nature of the work between an established firm and a sole practitioner—a rapidly vanishing breed. Because of high overhead and skyrocketing malpractice premiums, most sole practitioners find it difficult to make a living, much less a fortune. The economics of law practice over the past twenty years have dictated the development of ever-larger law firms with more and more branches. Partners will earn several orders of magnitude more than sole practitioners and attend to corporate clients rather than individuals. Partners likely negotiate and oversee various business deals while the sole practitioner performs a wide range of services from divorces through personal injuries. The disappearance of the sole practitioner is not good news for women lawyers, many of whom choose this more flexible option while raising a family.

In between large firm partners and sole practitioners are judges, law professors, government attorneys, in-house corporate counsels, and public interest law firms. While judges and law professors command great respect, they are relatively few in number. Choosing an alternative legal track among the remaining options has serious financial consequences.[36] Of legal jobs requiring bar passage, private practice paid the highest median at $90,000, while larger firms are known to pay up to at least $125,000 for first-year attorneys. Corporate counsel or business law jobs were second in pay at $60,000. Government and public interest jobs paid the lowest at $41,548 and $36,000 respectively.[37] None of these options compete with private law firms in the race to riches, but most offer more of another precious commodity: time.

Corporate law departments in large companies are the best-paid alternatives to law firms. According to a recent study, *Better on Balance,* a significant number of men and women attorneys leave law firms to seek "lifestyle changes" or a "better balance of work and family."[38] Many are disappointed. Hoping to secure fifty-hour workweeks and free weekends, these corporate lawyers often find that law firm hours have invaded the corporate environment as well. And the same stigma that plagues the part-timer in law firms also prevails in many corporate law departments.

Public interest law, pursued more often by women than men, is in a category of its own. Many young law students, passionate about social justice issues, train specifically to use their tools to advance a cause. Dedicated students aspire to make a difference in the world as champions for an idea or a population—underserved children, battered women, global peace. They are often bitterly disappointed to find few paying jobs in this sector and more attorneys competing for them than for the more lucrative positions with firms. The public interest jobs that do exist rarely pay a decent salary.

Hilary Ronen is a public interest lawyer in charge of legal services for the San Francisco Day Labor Program at La Raza Central in San Francisco's Mission district. We met at a dim bohemian coffee bar across the street from her office where the vegetarian menu and large piles of activist pamphlets draw a young, politically conscious crowd. Hilary's outfit, a down-to-earth dress reminiscent of the 1960s, would have been unthinkable in the buttoned-down, corporate office environments of private law. Despite these surface differences, Hilary's drive, passion, and commitment are cut from the same cloth as all those women in the private firm fast track. "After completing my law degree I realized my heart was really in community organizing, but I wanted to make use of my degree and needed to in order to get the loan repayment from Berkeley. This position allows me to incorporate both." Her schedule varies depending on what litigation is scheduled, but Hilary says her workday is usually around nine hours—far fewer than the number of hours worked by many associates and partners in private firms. Still, she believes the job would be difficult with children. In her office there is only one woman with a child, and Hilary noted that she works less than everyone else because she's often pulled away from the office by family commitments, such as medical appointments and baseball games. "It makes a big difference. You can't throw yourself into the job the way you want to when you have a kid."

Hilary plans to have children but finds it difficult to see how she can make it work. Her husband, who immigrated from the Dominican Republic three years ago, has yet to find stable employment. Still, Hilary believes the non-profit environment is more amenable to accommodating babies. Her law school mentor brought her own newborn baby to work with her everyday. "She set up a crib in her office and would even take her to meetings. She and her baby were so close it was amazing." Hilary believes this flexibility to be a mother *and* a working professional is one of the big perks of nonprofit work. "I have too much passion and energy to not work."

Hilary does not feel that she is in a second tier. She has overcome great odds to succeed in public interest law. Still, she recognizes that her position and financial situation are fragile, and family obligations might derail her. "I am sounding extremely confident right now but I worry sometimes about my future and not having the right skills to make enough money, and what would happen if someone got hurt or sick, or if I will need to take care of my parents when they are older, and when I have a family if I will be able to support them. I calm myself thinking, well, I did not have money when I was growing up."

Although career driven, Hilary is keenly aware that her dedication to her work could easily overshadow family life—a trap she doesn't want to fall into. "All my heroes growing up were world-renowned activists and community organizers such as Che Guevara, Nelson Mandela, and Subcomandante Marcos. They were all really marginal as parents, if not worse . . . I went to law school not because I care about the law; I care about justice. But I will not give up family."

GYPSY SCHOLARS IN THE UNIVERSITY

Two offices in my department have two or three faculty names on the door displayed on temporary cardboard cards. These are the offices of the part-time faculty, the lecturers who teach one or two courses. Over the years I have met a few of them, usually in the hallway or the mailroom. I have never seen them at a faculty meeting or department party, even though some of them have been teaching in the department for ten or more years. Some of them are among the best teachers in the department, according to student evaluations.

Part-time and adjunct faculty are by definition academics who are not on a tenure track and never receive the status or security of a professor. They are the fastest-growing segment of employees in academia. Again, this temporary track is overpopulated with women, usually women with children. A major reason for the rapid growth of temporary faculty is that hiring a temporary lecturer involves less expense and greater flexibility, and there are increasing numbers of women Ph.D.'s, particularly mothers, who will take the jobs. Our studies of women Ph.D.'s with children revealed that they are about twice as likely than men with children to fall into this second tier.[39] Sometimes they choose this tier because they are part of a dual career couple. The partner's (usually the husband's) position prevails and they accept a lesser job in order to accommodate the partner's career. Women also make this compromise in order to choose where they live and to be near family. Often they believe they will return to full-time when their children are older.

As a part-time lecturer for many years, I can attest that the pay was remarkably low and the benefits and security nonexistent. A lecturer would not know, often until the last moment, whether there were sufficient funds to pay for his or her job. Tenure-rank faculty always had first cut, and the leftovers (if there were any) were offered to second tier faculty. I was one of the lucky few part-timers who reentered the fast track, and I was able to do so largely because I had written (what turned out to be) an important book. Such instances are rare. Lecturers in the second tier almost never compete for a position in the tenure track; their years in the second tier automatically discount their eligibility as scholars qualified for the first tier. The insecurity and poor pay often force lecturers into a life on the road, seeking new employment or a second job—the gypsy scholar.

Who Gets Tenure*

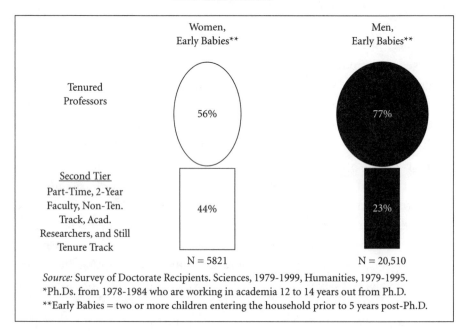

	Women, Early Babies**	Men, Early Babies**
Tenured Professors	56%	77%
<u>Second Tier</u> Part-Time, 2-Year Faculty, Non-Ten. Track, Acad. Researchers, and Still Tenure Track	44%	23%
	N = 5821	N = 20,510

Source: Survey of Doctorate Recipients. Sciences, 1979-1999, Humanities, 1979-1995.
*Ph.Ds. from 1978-1984 who are working in academia 12 to 14 years out from Ph.D.
**Early Babies = two or more children entering the household prior to 5 years post-Ph.D.

Conditions have improved somewhat at many universities with the unionization of lecturers, which has provided a limited degree of security and a better chance of securing health benefits. As with all second tiers, the hours are more manageable. Part-time and temporary positions do not come with high expectations of research and publication, which is the back breaker for tenure track professions. Still, among the professions, the second tier of academia offers the fewest advantages for women—or men.

Leslie Zwillinger, a long-term university lecturer, grew up in apartheid South Africa during the politically charged 1950s. She decided to leave after witnessing several riots and seeing friends taken away by police. Leslie obtained a visitor's visa to the United States and applied to doctoral programs in order to extend her visa to a longer-term student visa. "I started a counseling program at SF State. I went because it was available, not because it was ideal. My career direction has been more happenstance than deliberate, which is probably one of the bigger mistakes but it is what I needed to do to stay in the country."

Leslie soon met her husband, Gene, who was teaching classes at SF State at the time. While working on her doctorate in special education, Leslie had two children and also began to lecture part-time. Ultimately she ran into the "nepotism wall," which is a sometimes formal and more often informal rule that universities should not hire the spouse of faculty in the same department.

"My time base built up from 20 percent to 50 percent and 100 percent with grants and would cut back when there were funding cuts. I have been 100 percent time for a long time now. It is very clear to many of us part-time people in the academic system that it is not a good route to a tenure track position. Departments tend to hire new blood.

"The majority of part-timers are women who stay at 40 percent FTE [full-time equivalent] for the benefits. For these lifers it's always a struggle and always a battle. Their job is very insecure and very uncomfortable. One part-timer just retired because after twenty years of teaching, the schedule came out and her name just was not there. No one talked to her or discussed anything. She did end up teaching the class but she was fed up and decided she was just done with it. This is someone who was a vital part of the department."

Part-time lecturers and adjunct faculty are often overqualified and underpaid but, given that tenure track academic jobs are notoriously scarce, some Ph.D.'s see these positions as their only chance to stay in their field or attached to a scholarly environment. Adjuncts and part-timers may never gain faculty status or participate in faculty committees, but if the alternative is a complete exit from the academic environment, these marginalized positions are, in their minds, a better option.

Across all fast track professions, part-time workers rarely retain the same status they enjoyed as full-timers, and often their colleagues resent them because they are not always available. In universities, some other faculty member will have to pick up an additional course, in the publishing world, another editor will have to stay late for the deadline. Part-timers are no longer seen as colleagues but as problems. When it comes time to confer tenure, partnership, or the next big step up the ladder, they may be passed by.

Because they fear these consequences, many mothers avoid part-time tracks, even when they desperately need them. Our study of University of California faculty revealed that a majority of mothers who were eligible for a reduced load—effectively no teaching for a semester following childbirth—did not take advantage of the benefit. They said they chose not do so for fear of their colleagues' disapproval. Not surprisingly, women who had already achieved tenure, who had successfully completed their probationary period, were more likely to take the part-time break.[40]

THE HOLY GRAIL: PART-TIME FLEXIBLE TRACKS

Part-time positions with the right to reenter the full-time track have been the holy grail of work/family activists since the 1970s. And like the holy grail they continue to be elusive. Felicia Schwartz, a successful corporate executive who worked part-time for several years when her three children were young, went on to found Catalyst, an advocacy organization for women in business. She recommended, based on her own experience, that a slower career path could be a win-win proposition. Mothers would not be forced out of their professions, children would get more attention in their early years, and employers wouldn't lose talented employees. Her 1989 article in the *Harvard Business Review* promoting a temporary part-time arrangement provoked a bitter debate. The idea was derisively dubbed a "mommy track" (not a term she used) and ridiculed by employers and feminists alike. At the time, many feminists opposed Schwartz's idea because they feared it would lead to a permanent second tier within organizations; it would be yet another way of sidelining women, permanently restricting them to a subordinate role.[41]

Regrettably, the record on part-time tracks so far has verified this prediction. Part-time tracks of any kind are still rare in the corporate world and are often given arbitrarily. Even though studies have shown that flexible family-friendly policies will improve productivity, the corporate world, for the most part, is still committed to a one-size-fits-all workplace.

In one study, a mother took a leave of absence to attend to a child's medical problem and when she returned she tried for a part-time position. "I went back to talk to them about what was next, and a part-time situation presented itself in the sales area, and I got all gung-ho for that. I got all the child care arrangements in place, started interviewing people to watch the kids, and at the last minute the big boss wouldn't sign off on it."[42] The woman chose instead to leave altogether. Indeed, according to the U.S. census, one in four women quit their jobs shortly before or after childbirth.[43]

However, part-time tracks, when implemented correctly, can deliver on their promise. Angela, a health care analyst and mother of two, was able to negotiate a four-day week and flexible schedule with the opportunity to return to full-time when ready. Other mothers at her workplace have used the flexible schedule option for up to a year after their maternity leave, and they have still managed to move up the corporate ladder to management positions. This arrangement creates a win-win for the company and women employees: the firm retains key talent and the working mothers can take a breather during the toughest years of child rearing without having to abandon their careers completely.

Medicine also offers better models. As previously observed, women doctors have more children than women lawyers, corporate executives, and professors, and they are much less likely to drop out of their profession. There is an acceptance of a reduced-hour schedule, especially in group practices and in large HMOs like Kaiser. Though such positions are usually the lowest-paying and least prestigious specialties, women doctors have the ability to move from part-time to full-time, a choice rarely possible in other professions. These tracks may not be the most esteemed tier in the profession, and they are definitely not as well paid, but they offer a comfortable alternative.[44]

The availability of flexible part-time tracks with the ability to return to full-time when desired is the most important workplace reform needed by fast track mothers. Conquering this frontier requires not just new policies but a shift in the workplace culture. Employers and coworkers must be convinced that it's good for productivity and the bottom line to retain some of the best and brightest new professionals. We are advancing these arguments in the university world, using the information from our Do Babies Matter? research project to make the case that we are needlessly losing some of our rising stars, the graduate students for whom we had high hopes. Thus far we have made some serious progress in implementing more family leave and part-time tenure track options. In the last chapter we will return to this elusive goal.

6

Beyond the Glass Ceiling: Forty to Sixty-Five and Beyond

You have to be like a phoenix. You must rise from your own ashes. You will make mistakes but you have to be able to come back. You have to know your staying power and nurture it.
—Senator Dianne Feinstein

As the only woman dean at Berkeley for several years, I sat in on countless meetings where men held the floor. One day a woman colleague made a presentation to a deans' meeting and received a cursory, almost rude response. Afterward she asked me how she could have been more effective. "Speak lowly and slowly, but smile frequently," I replied.

This advice (which did help her next presentation) was based on my observation that women must adhere to a narrow band of behavior in order to be effective in mostly male settings. Women who speak too fast or in a shrill tone are overlooked. Women who act in a highly assertive manner, which might be acceptable for men, are attended to but not invited back. Women must be friendly but not too friendly, or a sexual connotation may be inferred.

Navigating this male-dominated world can be disorienting and stressful. The real question is, Why aren't there more of us at the table?

As we have seen, some women slip off the fast track, most often because of family conflicts, and fail to reach the most rewarding and productive period of their careers. Those who persevere through the grueling make-or-break years and move forward in their profession are able to enjoy the heart of their career—the twenty-five to thirty years before retirement. They achieve relative security, good positions, higher pay, and institutional seniority: tenured professor, chief of staff, law partner, and senior editor. Most will live out their career lives in a productive mode, taking on more responsibility and achieving greater recognition.

But even these persistent, successful women will fall short of reaching the very top leadership positions in their field, and most won't be paid equitably. In all of these professions there is a well-documented disparity between the pay that senior men and senior women receive. Women earn seventy-two cents on the male dollar in executive corporate America.[1] Women partners in law firms take home sixty-eight cents,[2] and women doctors earn sixty-five cents on the dollar compared with men.[3]

Twenty years ago the *Wall Street Journal* coined the term "glass ceiling" to describe the apparent barriers that prevent women from reaching the top of the corporate hierarchy. In 1995 the government's Glass Ceiling Commission reported that women had 45.7 percent of America's jobs and received more than half of university master's degrees. Yet 95 percent of senior managers were men, and female managers' earnings were on average a scant 68 percent of their male counterparts'. A decade later, women account for 46.5 percent of America's workforce and represent less than 8 percent of its top managers (although at large Fortune 500 companies the figure is slightly higher).[4] Female managers' earnings now average 72 percent of their male colleagues' wages. Since 1998 the figures have stagnated. Overall, the trajectory is not promising.

In other professions, the elusive top leadership positions are sometimes referred to as the "second glass ceiling," acknowledging that while many women have achieved powerful positions that were originally beyond their grasp—professor, partner, editor—many more have failed to rise to the pinnacle leadership positions.

THE KINGS OF THE HILL

It is not always clear who is included among those at the very top in other fast-track professions as it is in business with the definitive pecking order of CEO, CFO, and chairman of the board of a Fortune 500 company—titles that normally reflect the salary scale. Is the heart surgeon who invents new techniques and earns a large salary above the dean of the medical school? Is a Nobel Prize winner more powerful than a university president? But no matter which criterion you use—fame, fortune, or power—there are relatively few women in these top positions. Only 5 percent of managing partners in large law firms are women,[5] less than 10 percent of medical school deans are women,[6] and just 9 percent of National Academy of Science members—the elite group which represents the pinnacle of prestige for scientists.[7] And women who hold respectable ranks just under these top positions—law partner, full professor, chief of staff—are still fewer in number and paid less than men in similar positions.

Gender discrimination is the usual explanation for this pattern of disparities. There are indeed pockets of the corporate world, particularly in finance, where the climate is overtly hostile to women. A recent well-publicized federal lawsuit brought by women stockbrokers at Merrill Lynch revealed a male world where women were routinely passed over for promotions and subjected to sexual harassment.[8]

Another, more subtle factor may be that women are left out of job-related social networking. Jock talk and all-night boozing reputedly make the wheels of industry turn, and men supposedly feel more comfortable in the company of other men. A 2003 Catalyst survey of women in corporate leadership positions found that 41 percent of respondents cited "exclusion from informal networks" as a barrier to their overall advancement.[9]

Often subtle discrimination is rooted in gender stereotypes—especially when it comes to the "leadership issue." Women are purportedly passed up for promotions based on a conscious or unconscious belief that women do not have what it takes to lead men. The English have a test for this kind of leadership: "Who among you would kill the tiger if attacked?"

But a woman who displays the qualities of a "tiger killer" is chastised for being "too masculine." This paradox was the subject of a landmark 1989 Supreme Court case, *Price Waterhouse v. Hopkins*. Ann Hopkins was turned down for a promotion on a split decision of all male partners who evaluated her performance. A number of these evaluations sharply criticized her interpersonal skills and specifically called her too abrasive. Several of the evaluations on both sides made comments implying that Hopkins "was or had been acting masculine," and one partner advised her that "she could improve her chances for partnership by walking, talking, and dressing more femininely."[10] After the partners in her office refused to reconsider her for partnership the next year, Hopkins resigned and brought an action against the firm in the U.S. District Court for the District of Columbia. Ultimately she prevailed before the U.S. Supreme Court.

Women like Ann Hopkins clearly are driven to reach the top of their profession. But some controversial studies have cast doubt on whether most women really want to ascend to the highest rungs of the career ladder or at least point to their ambivalence about the issue. A 2002 survey of top executives in American multinational companies around the world did find women to be less ambitious, at least about achieving the very top job: 19 percent of the men interviewed aspired to be CEO, whereas only 9 percent of the women did.[11] On the other hand, Catalyst, the organization most responsible for tracking women's experience in business, has shown that women and men have equal desires to have the CEO job.[12] Surveys like this are inevitably limited by the reality that women see few role models at the top or even near the top. And those women who are at the top, like my female professors at Vassar forty years ago, probably do not have families.

A closer look at the top executives of the Fortune 500 companies offers dramatic contrasts in family situations and attitudes about family. Catalysts's recent survey of Fortune 1000 CEOs and women executives at the vice president level and above reveals that 67 percent of female executives, but only 35 percent of CEOs (almost all male), hold the perception that commitment to personal or family responsibilities is a barrier to advancement in the business profession.[13] Surveying the field of top executives within three levels of CEO, family configurations reflect an even greater imbalance. Forty-nine percent of women are married with children, compared to 84 percent of men. More striking is how these couples handle their work lives. The largest study of global executives on work–life issues reveals that 74 percent of the women surveyed have a spouse or partner who is employed full-time, while 75 percent of men surveyed have a spouse or partner who is not employed at all.[14] Gender differences also emerge in planning for children. A 2003 study by the Families and Work Institute found that 35 percent of executive women, versus 12 percent of executive men, said they had delayed having children and 12 percent of women versus 1 percent of men decided not to have children at all.[15]

The explanations frequently offered for women's lack of corporate success are commonly put forward for the other professions as well. Entry-level positions in science and engineering at prestigious universities are publicly advertised, but most often they will pass on to the heir apparent, an established scientist, almost always a male, who is well connected with professors in that department. The few women who are hired into these elite positions often face an unfair work environment. In 1999 the Massachusetts Institute of Technology (MIT) issued a report acknowledging that its distinguished women full professors (only sixteen) suffer from pervasive, if unintentional, discrimination in hiring, awards, promotion, in the allocation of laboratory space and research funds, and in representation on important committees.[16] This came as a wake-up call to the university, which apparently thought, as do most male scientists when surveyed, that the days of discrimination were over. Women who receive Ph.D.s are less likely than men to follow research careers at major universities. In mathematics, 46 percent of graduating undergraduates are women, but only 8 percent of math faculty are women, according to the Institute for Research on Women and Gender at Stanford University.[17] Overall, men still hold most of the senior ranked positions in science and engineering research and academic positions.[18] Women who do persist earn less and are promoted less frequently to senior academic ranks than their male counterparts.[19]

Claudia Henrion, author of *Women in Mathematics: The Addition of Difference,* notes that about 60 percent of female faculty do not have children compared with about 30 percent of male professors. "The cost we're asking women to pursue this path is extremely high," she said. "They're being asked to choose in a way most men are not asked to choose. Until that gets addressed, it's a real disincentive for a lot of women," she said in an interview with the *Stanford Review.*[20]

In the field of law, women are excluded from social opportunities that help their male counterparts get ahead. Partners play golf with clients to bring in business and it becomes the basis for personal friendships and future work. While men frequently reference each other's previous comments in building their arguments, women's contributions are overlooked. Women are perceived as less willing to give it their all, not willing to kill the tiger.

Most mothers experience more than one of these restraints during their career. It is usually an accumulation of setbacks that holds them back. I call this the "snowwoman effect." The layers of missed opportunities, family obligations, and small and large slights build up over the years, slowing their career progress compared with men. Virginia Valian, in her insightful book *Why So Slow?* suggests that, like interest on capital, disadvantages accrue and accumulate, ultimately resulting in large disparities in salary promotion and prestige for women. Her work describes the psychological and institutional ways in which all women are treated differently from birth.[21] For mothers, family constraints impede career progress in addition to the gender schemas, which slow all women down.

In most analyses of women's failure to penetrate the glass ceiling, family issues are sidelined in favor of amorphous gender discrimination explanations, even though across the professions, about 60 percent of women who persist on the fast track after the make-or-break years are mothers. This holds true for women executives, tenured professors, and members of the National Academy of Sciences.[22] Some note is given to the fact that women who leave to have children have a difficult time getting back on track, and occasionally elder care is mentioned. Women, more than men, are sometimes called on for extended care of failing parents. Indeed, women who make it past the make-or-break years and successfully raise families while excelling in their careers often face a new, equally daunting challenge in their forties and fifties—caring for aging parents. In the Work–Life Policy study, 24 percent of highly qualified women reported the demands of caring for elderly parents as a factor that pulled them away from their jobs.[23]

Professional women also are far more likely than men to experience the disruption of divorce, which can affect their ability to perform for years.[24] Likewise, growing families are unpredictable; troubled teens may need more attention than they did at an earlier age, and sick relatives may need extended care.

In all fast track professions, marriage and children appear to boost men's careers and slow or stop women's. A recent study of the career progression of men and women MBAs over the course of the 1990s found that family situations, including periods of work interruptions and work reductions, played the most important role in holding women back.[25]

Across professions, the lack of women role models in top leadership positions is problematic. It is not just a problem for young women who aspire to the top but see few women ahead of them; it is a problem for those at the top as well. A study of women doctors in academia found that "women who do persevere and advance face the extra challenge of 'surplus visibility.'" Because the higher they go, the fewer they are, women become ever more exceptional by their mere presence on the academic scene and visible to the point of inviting critical scrutiny. While this visibility can represent an opportunity, living in a "glass house" with no room for error is more often a problem.[26]

THE RIGHT STUFF

These facts and figures paint a picture of gloom and doom for career mothers, and yet in spite of it all, driven and talented women are at the top—Nancy

Pelosi, grandmother and first female Speaker of the House, Meg Whitman, CEO of eBay, and Susan Hockfield, president of MIT, to name a few. These resilient women have weathered the most difficult period when family and work are the most demanding and reached the pinnacle of their professions.

And there are young women rising through the ranks close behind these pioneers, striving to reach the top of their respective careers. These women at the top serve as important role models for this next generation, and their experiences provide us with important life lessons about how to have it all—family, career, *and* success.

SUPPORT NETWORKS

Senator Dianne Feinstein is one of the most influential women in the United States. She began opening doors before the pioneer generation knocked on them in the 1970s. She became the "first" in many positions: first woman president of the San Francisco Board of Supervisors, first woman mayor of San Francisco, first woman U.S. senator from California, first woman to be on the Judiciary Committee, and first woman on the Energy and Water Board of Appropriations. As senator she has taken bold stands on such critical issues as gun control and identity theft—not necessarily women's issues, but in keeping with her general focus on consumer health and safety.

In our interview, Senator Feinstein—still working at a hectic pace after four decades of public service—recounted her difficult road as a high-powered working mother. As for almost all of the successful mothers we interviewed, finding the right partner was critical to her success. "I don't believe I could have done it without that stability and support.... unless you have very good full-time help you can't manage your hours yourself," she says. This claim is reinforced by research suggesting that unsupportive partners create barriers to women's success. The work–life policy study on highly qualified women found that 40 percent of married respondents said they felt their spouses create more work around the house than they perform.[27] Excelling in a career can easily be stymied by a crushing second shift at home, made worse by a spouse who doesn't contribute to the housework or undervalues his wife's career. Feinstein, however, was lucky to have a partner who offered financial and emotional support—a foundation that allowed her to succeed in politics.

This theme is also often mentioned by women members of the National Academy of Sciences, whom Elga Wasserman interviews in her insightful book, *The Door in the Dream*. One scientist bluntly advised, "If a husband does not support his wife's career as a scientist, the wife as only two choices— give up her career or give up the husband."[28]

In addition to partners, successful women often give credit to a strong support network. Mentors who encouraged them at critical times in their child-raising years were critical. One scientist, for example, was given the rare flexibility to slow down during the make-or-break years without penalty. "My chairman at the time when I had four children under the age of seven years offered me the opportunity of reducing my commitment to the department for a few years while leaving me all the dignity of a well-accepted and integrated member of the department and the certainty that I would get into the regular tenure-accruing track when I was ready. He did this in such a way that my colleagues were, for the most part, unaware that I was in a special position and thus accepted me as an equal colleague."[29]

STAY IN THE GAME

Women who make it to the top rarely take extended time off, even when continuing to work is at its most challenging. Senator Feinstein briefly put aside her political ambitions following the birth of her daughter and a difficult divorce. Nonetheless she remained open to political opportunities. "I had very little money and I had to make my way with great difficulty. While I was on my own working in the industrial welfare commission, Governor Pat Brown asked me if I would be a member of the California Women's Board of Terms and Parole. I had to be in Los Angeles nine days a month. It was good money and I could pay my rent, but I had to also pay for someone to stay with my daughter. That was the hardest time of my life. She was three years old and I was on my own."

Congresswoman Zoe Lofgren, who represents California's 16th District (San Jose), was elected in 1981 and became pregnant soon after. She was the first woman supervisor to have a baby while in office. "I had a C-section and was out for two weeks, but there was no such thing as maternity leave for elected officials. If I was not there, my constituents were not represented," she said. In order to stay in the game Lofgren came up with some creative work arrangements: "On Tuesdays my mother would help me. I would go into the office with my mother and [daughter] and she would keep her up in my office. When she needed to be fed, I would get called out [of meetings] and it was like, 'hold the vote—I will be right back!' "

In spite of the conflicting demands, Lofgren had her second child three years later and continued her political life as supervisor while participating in the PTA and going on school field trips. "I would go on the field trips not just for the kids but because it was fun to be a mom. I did not want to miss out on motherhood either. You can cut corners in some ways (it's not as important that the house gets cleaned), but sitting down to dinner as a family is everything."

Still, when the opportunity arose, Lofgren ran for and won a seat in Congress, which meant moving to Washington. Her family did not want to leave California, and when the children were ten and fourteen Lofgren became a bicoastal mom, as she still is today. While she is away from home, Lofgren puts in long, strenuous hours: "There was a time that I was in D.C. and I was working until 2:00 A.M. every evening."

Lofgren's story is powerful and unusual. One of the main reasons there are so few mothers in national politics is that a member of the Senate or the House of Representatives must live in both his or her constituency and in Washington. It is commonplace for congressmen and senators to share an apartment in Washington with other members of Congress, while maintaining their families elsewhere in the country and returning home on weekends. The reluctance to move for job advantage is one of the reasons that women lag behind men in obtaining these top positions.

In spite of the trade-offs it requires, Lofgren believes taking on motherhood and a high-profile career has its advantages. "I think making a contribution to the well-being of society in the public and political arena is an important thing. I think that to do that in order to forgo a wanted motherhood you would be making a terrible mistake. The greatest education I ever had was becoming a mother. It transformed my outlook on life; I understood what is important not just for me but also for society."

Judith Klinman, my colleague at Berkeley, followed a similar path. She is one of very few women to ascend to the National Academy of Sciences, a universally recognized marker of professional success. In the star system of science, it is an exclusive guild—only sixty new members are elected each year. Women, who represent only 9 percent of members, form an even more exclusive club within that guild.[30]

Klinman had children while she was still a graduate student and then followed her husband's opportunities, making a place for her own research as best as she could. This included shifts from 3:00 to 4:00 A.M. as a graduate student while her infant son slept. In spite of these challenges, she persisted and secured her first job with a government-sponsored research laboratory, a less demanding track than a university appointment. For a good part of her career she managed as a single parent, but she did not have to deal with teaching and tenure during her make-or-break years. In spite of a divorce and having to raise two adolescent sons on her own, Klinman made steady progress on her research and was hired at Berkeley in 1978 as an already tenured professor.

For these women, persistence and energy during the make-or-break period resulted in later career success.

TIME MANAGEMENT FOR THE LIFECOURSE

Arguably, the life of a politician is among the most demanding routes on the fast track. Campaigning and fund-raising are constant requirements and the travel and time away from home take a toll on family life. During the nine years that Feinstein was mayor of San Francisco, her hours increased dramatically and she arranged her schedule creatively around family commitments. "I worked long days but I limited my nights out to three or four a week and that worked well for me." On her nights at home, Mayor Feinstein would catch up on office work, often studying various issues for three to four hours every evening.

According to a colleague of Mary K. Bunting, the future president of Radcliffe, Bunting would come to the lab after 7:00 P.M. each evening after her physician husband took over the care of their four children. And for my Berkeley colleague, Judith Klinman, managing time and tasks strategically were key to her success, as was the timing of her two children. "I did not really begin my most important research until my youngest child left home—when I was already in my forties. Then I had the time and energy to really devote to it."

CONTROL BURNOUT

Dede Bartlett was among the first women to enter the corporate inner sanc-
tums. I first met Dede at our Vassar reunion a few years ago. Other classmates
had told me that she was our class "corporate success story." At our meeting,
Dede, like almost all successful women I have met, did not think she was
different from other women she knew. She made light of both her struggles
and her successes. Yet she is very aware that her daughter's generation has a
daunting future; in her opinion, there are more obstacles to overcome in the
new high-speed corporate environment.

A French major in college, Dede found her first job with a small firm in
marketing. Her talent for sales, writing, and speaking were quickly recognized
on her next job with a public relations firm, and she became a vice president
at twenty-seven. Hired by Mobil in the early 1970s as a public relations expert,
Dede rapidly ascended the corporate ladder, in part because new civil rights
legislation required companies to increase the female presence in management positions.

While demanding, the corporate schedule was not so difficult for Dede to
manage, particularly since she had a supportive husband and a mother and
mother-in-law who could pitch in during emergencies. Today, corporate VPs
rarely adhere to a 9-to-5 schedule but in the early days of Dede's career, she
made it home every night by 6:30 to have dinner with her family. But when
Mobil moved to Virginia, Dede decided to stay in New York in order to accommodate her husband's career. Fortunately her experience allowed her to
move to another Fortune 10 corporation—Phillip Morris.

But the new work environment included higher pressure and longer hours.
"The level and pace of the work changed. Phillip Morris was a much more
aggressive company and my department was run by the general counsel, who
was overseeing a number of high-profile lawsuits. At the time my daughter
had one more year before going to boarding school and my son had three
years before boarding school ... The pace of my work was such that it was
really getting to be tough to balance work and family."

According to Dede, the workplace grew even more demanding with the
advent of e-mail, cell phones, and other technology that increased productivity. "There were extraordinary dynamic changes in culture that made life
very difficult. The digital revolution happened in 1995. E-mail came along,

and with that came a dramatic pickup in the level of work. When I left in 2002 I became convinced that the pace of work was so grindingly tough—with the late nights and weekends—that it would be impossible to have the quality of family life I had experienced with my kids when they were younger. The prime reason for me taking early retirement was due to my family—I had never walked out of a work-related situation before, but I knew I would probably barely make it to my daughter's wedding or son's graduation if I did not leave." Retiring in their late fifties is not unusual for corporate executives, but Dede's decision was based on the burnout factor noted by Dianne Feinstein and other highly successful mothers. Mothers experience burnout at a higher rate than other employees and they are more likely to leave the game earlier than men. Nearly half of working women of the baby boomer generation will be out of the labor force before their sixty-second birthday, while only one-third of men will.[31]

The ever-increasing demands of the workplace and the speedup of productivity threaten the ability of the next generation of women to handle both work and family. Successful ABC lead news anchor Elizabeth Vargas, forty-three, was on the fast track to become the next Katie Couric when she announced in 2006 that she would step down to take care of her children. Vargas said her unexpected departure was a result of the around-the-clock requirements of the job—and the demands of being the mother of a three-year-old with another child on the way.

As Senator Dianne Feinstein notes, recognizing burnout and learning how to deal with it is an important characteristic of successful women. "You have to listen to yourself. The key to a successful career is to be able to do it for fifty years," she said. "What I see with so many women is that just as they are being trusted and becoming vital, knowledgeable, and consistent, they do not stay the course; they get worn out. It is essential to know the speed you can go at. I often say to women, 'You have to be like a Phoenix—you must rise from your own ashes. You will make mistakes, but you have to be able to come back. You have to know your staying power and nurture it, and some people do not know how.'"

As Klinman, the Berkeley chemistry professor, notes, pacing yourself and realizing that there is a light at the end of the tunnel after the make-or-break years can be key to career success.

PLAN STRATEGICALLY

After leaving the corporate world, Dede Bartlett became the chair of the Advisory Council of the National Domestic Violence Hotline. In addition, she consults on domestic violence issues for nonprofit organizations, corporations, and government agencies. She is also past president of the Women's Forum. Part of the forum's mission is to bring young women up the ranks to fill executive vacancies. Drawing on the lessons learned from her own experience, Dede advises young women to arm themselves with an MBA and make strategic decisions early on if they want to climb the corporate ladder.

In order to survive in today's fast-paced, bottom line–driven business environment, women should choose their line of work carefully, she says. "You want to avoid staff positions like human resources and public relations. If you really are serious about advancing in major corporate positions, you want to get into a line position; you want to have profit and loss responsibilities. You want to be in charge of something that produces revenue for the company."

Bartlett also believes mothers, if they plan wisely, can make use of part-time options for a number of years and still remain in the game. "The name of the game in rising in any corporation is visibility. Part-time work allows you to keep your network of contacts current, your skills up-to-date and your work visible with people who can help you. You need to remember that you will always be competing with women who have decided to remain in the workforce full-time, so you will be off that fast track. But if you managed to be strategic in how you prepared your career before that, then I think you stand a good shot a getting back on the on ramp."

ADVOCATE FOR YOUR RIGHTS

When my colleague Judith Klinman was hired, she was the first woman faculty member in the Chemistry Department, indeed in the physical sciences. Later in her career, shortly after being elected to the National Academy of Sciences, she learned that she was being paid significantly less than her male peers in the department. "The expectation was that I would be a good mother and a good teacher and not rock the boat too much." But Klinman did rock the boat and rose to the top ranks. She focused on her research, was promoted to senior faculty, and served as the department chair (the only woman to do so).

At times motherhood itself—and the stereotypes associated with it—can lead to workplace discrimination. When women demonstrate highly feminine behavior, like becoming pregnant, they may elicit emotional reactions that reflect a different kind of gender stereotyping. Men may become protective and unwilling to allow the mother to engage in activities that are not mother centered.

Many theorists claim that all gender discrimination is, fundamentally, maternal discrimination. The ideal feminine stereotype is the ideal mother—nurturing, self-effacing, and, above all, submissive to the male protector. Even sexual harassment can be interpreted as an aggressive male action to keep a woman under control.

Joan Williams, a pioneer in the growing field of maternal discrimination lawsuits, notes that sometimes employers who don't think of themselves as holding gender bias may suddenly change their behavior after an employee becomes pregnant.

Elana Black, a child psychologist in Buffalo, New York, brought a lawsuit against her employer, a public elementary school, in 2004 after her supervisors allegedly denied her tenure because she is a mother. Black alleged that after the birth of her first child, school district officials began pressuring her to reconsider whether she could be a mother and do her job. They argued that the position's long hours and complex responsibilities were inappropriate for someone with young children.[32] Such cases, while rare, have increased dramatically over the past thirty years. Between 1970 and 1975 just two caregiver discrimination lawsuits were filed, while 182 were filed between 2000 and 2005.[33]

But men become victims of maternal discrimination as well. As breadwinners they are encouraged to work even longer hours once they have family responsibilities, and discouraged from taking time off to attend to childbirth or child-raising obligations.[34] Gender stereotyping can be punitive for fathers as well as mothers. Joan Williams notes that in one lawsuit, an employer told a father he could not take parental leave because he could not be considered the primary caretaker unless his wife was "in a coma or dead." Men are penalized for taking on what is considered a feminine role and women are penalized if they refuse to play the role as prescribed.[35]

Not all prescriptive stereotyping is hostile. Another boss who employed both the mother and the father sent the mother home early and insisted the father stay later, presumably so he could better support his family. While benevolent in intent, the result disadvantaged both parents by infringing on their ability to determine their own family–career balance.[36]

At heart, gender discrimination and family restraints are not competing theories. The patterns of discrimination claimed by women who have won major lawsuits are not usually about mothers, but maternal discrimination is a component in all gender discrimination; sometimes it is the main component.

Most of the groundbreaking Title VII lawsuits that opened law firms, corporations, and universities to women were won by revealing clear patterns of gender exclusion and discrimination in hiring and promoting across the industry. Individual plaintiffs received the settlements, but the courts were making a statement about gender discrimination. Mothers were rarely plaintiffs in these suits, and issues of maternal discrimination were raised only in relation to general sex stereotyping.

Maternal discrimination cases are not easy to win. If a mother claims she is fired or not promoted because she cannot travel, the employer will claim business necessity—traveling is a requirement of the job. Most cases are won by claiming that the mother is willing to do what the job takes, but the employer will not give her the chance. While employers have learned to keep their mouths closed about sexist remarks and tiptoe carefully around any word or gesture that could be construed as sexual harassment, they are often remarkably frank when dealing with parenthood issues.

For example, attorney Joann Trezza, a mother of two young children, claimed she was passed over for promotion to managing attorney because she is a mother. In spite of the excellent evaluation she received, the job was offered to less qualified men with children and to a woman without children. She was told that she was not offered the position because the job required a good deal of traveling, and as a mother she would obviously not want that kind of schedule. In the course of the testimony it was also revealed that the senior VP of her company complained to her "about the incompetence and laziness of women who are also working mothers." Women in general, he complained, are not good planners and are "worse with kids." The court also considered that only seven out of forty-six managing attorneys were women, and none had school-age children, while many of the male managing partners did.[37]

Williams argues that winning lawsuits which give individual women a better chance to play the male game is not as effective as changing the rules of the game. Such lawsuits, she believes, should promote structural change—advancing flexible options for employees, particularly parents, which would not become permanent graveyards. She thinks there is a strong business case for making the best use of talent within an organization. She describes it as "the discrimination model mixed with the business case." The carrot is the most effective use of talent, and therefore greater productivity for the organization; the stick is the threat of liability.

SOMETHING LOST

Clearly we need more women in positions of power—women like Senator Feinstein, Congresswoman Lofgren, Dede Bartlett, and Judith Klinman who bring a woman's perspective to the most elite positions of power. We lose more than just role models when women are absent from this inner sanctum.

Bettina Plevan, the president of the New York City Bar Association, has argued that law firms lose out when there are few women at the top: "I think diversity is a beneficial thing in an organization. Without it, you have a loss of different points of view."[38]

Corporate America surely benefited from the perspectives of pioneering women like Dede Bartlett; the U.S. Congress and California constituents have benefited from the leadership and values of Senator Feinstein and Congresswoman Lofgren; and the scientific community—especially aspiring women scientists—have benefited from the groundbreaking work and leadership of Judith Klinman.

The dearth of women at the very top of the professions has profound implications. The U.S. Equal Opportunity Commission, taking note of gender disparities in law, noted in 2003, "Patterns of stratification within the legal profession are important in their own right . . . If race, gender, and social class are determinants for entry into the profession and for the attainment of certain positions within the profession, it may imply that these same attributes affect the sorts of treatment individuals will receive by legal institutions, in part because they do not have access to lawyers who share a similar social background."[39]

In medicine, the lack of women in leadership positions can lead to research and treatment priorities that are skewed toward men. Until recently, the predominantly male-focused cardiovascular research has been generalized to women and only in recent years have women been included in clinical trials or databases in sufficient numbers for sex-based analysis of the data.[40] As Dr. Karen Scott Collins, vice president of the Commonwealth Fund stated, "The gains of women help to contribute to an ongoing focus on women's health. What they bring is additional important concerns. For example, there is more focus on domestic violence as a medical problem, a lot of attention to counseling for menopause, a focus on reproductive health and so on."[41]

Much is at stake for women, for the professions, and for society as a whole when the positions of power and leadership become uniformly male. The lack of women at the top sends a distorted message to our undergraduate and graduate students, half of whom are female. They can expect equal treatment with men as students but not equal representation in the faculty or in other top leadership roles. It begs the question, Is equal treatment limited to the bottom of the pyramid?

Second Chances for Mothers on the Fast Track

Mothers who achieve the highest position in their field are wonderful models. Mothers serving as high court judges, university presidents, distinguished medical scientists, and corporate executives give courage to those starting up the ladder. They affirm that it is possible to have a family and a career, and they tell us that their lives are richer for having succeeded at both. We admire these mothers and greatly appreciate their work opening doors and holding them open for those who are following in their footsteps. But we also realize that these strong and determined women are walking a very narrow path, and a single slip—a divorce or a sick child—could permanently sideline them. To finish the revolution, we must level the playing field for mothers, so that not only the lucky and the strong can succeed. We must make it a family-friendly field where fathers play along alongside mothers. To do this, critical workplace changes are needed to remove the institutional barriers that sideline women.

Hard evidence can produce hard changes. At Berkeley, our Do Babies Matter? research project offered substantive proof that women were leaking out of the pipeline before taking their first academic positions. These talented young minds realized that if they stayed the course they would be at least forty before they achieved job security. They didn't see a way to fit children into that scenario. "I want a life more than I want a career," one of my students told me.

Our research, coupled with leadership from the University of California president, has led to a full-scale UC system–wide (ten universities) initiative, the UC Faculty Family Friendly Edge, which has begun to transform the academic culture. Both mothers and fathers can stop the tenure clock for up to one year to take time out for childbirth or adoption; both are eligible for one semester of teaching relief at full pay, mothers for two semesters. A part-time tenure track is available as well, which extends the tenure clock up to ten years.

Hiring faculty are encouraged to help place dual-career couples and dis-count "résumé gaps" when considering talented women—and men—who were diverted for a few years by family obligations. Rather than discarding them from the competition, search committees now consider the talent and potential of these nontraditional candidates. In addition, part-time emer-gency child care and more on-campus child care are in the planning stages.

At Berkeley we begin our initiatives with the graduate student years. Stop-ping the coursework clock, constructing new infant and toddler facilities, offering parent grants and paid maternity leave for supported students are important steps forward. Students are beginning to feel that it is safe to have children. Women students, in particular, are encouraged to stay the course.

Jenny Mitchell, a neuroscience postdoc, points out that such initiatives make it possible for young women, including graduate students, to start a fam-ily before assuming the crushing demands of a tenure track position. "When I was at Oregon Health Sciences University (OHSU) there were graduate stu-dents with children, and they got benefits and support for it. The attitude in the program was that it was an appropriate time to have a child because there's less pressure to publish." I believe these parental leave and "stop the clock" policies should be standard.

New options by themselves do not transform a culture; there must be encouragement, cooperation, and ongoing vigilance. In the university culture the department chair hires, monitors, and evaluates faculty performance. One of the initiatives in our Family Friendly Edge project is a "School for Chairs," which teaches these gatekeepers hiring and retention concepts such as actively promoting a second job for dual-career couples, discounting résumé gaps attributable to parenthood, ending faculty meetings by 5:00 P.M., and care-fully mentoring new parents through the tenure process. Most importantly, it is the chair's job to make the case at tenure time that stopping the clock and taking time off for childbearing cannot be used against otherwise qualified candidates.

These family-friendly policies are good business. They allow us to attract the best and brightest faculty and graduate students and to maintain our competitive edge. Our hiring rates for new women faculty at Berkeley have steadily climbed from 26 percent to nearly 40 percent over the past few years.

And other universities are clamoring to follow the lead. Institutions change when forced to compete with each other for the best talent. A recent meeting of the "nine presidents" (Harvard, Yale, Princeton, Stanford, MIT, University of Pennsylvania, University of Chicago, University of Michigan, and Berkeley) at UC Berkeley established benchmark criteria and a commitment to new policies by the presidents of all these universities.[1]

Beyond academia, some forward-looking countries are tackling these problems with sweeping policy reforms. In France, incentives offered by the government—including a three-year paid parental leave with guaranteed job protection on returning to the workforce; universal, full-time preschool starting at age three; subsidized day care before age three; stipends for in-home nannies; and monthly child care allowances—are changing the way professionals think about family. According to a recent report in the *Washington Post*, French mothers say they feel less guilt at work than their American counterparts do.[2] Marie-Therese Letablier, research director of the Center for Employment Studies, notes in the *Post* article that French policies have created a complete cultural paradigm shift. In many European countries it's "work or children," she says, while "in France, it's work and children." Letablier's statement is borne out by the numbers: three-quarters of all French mothers with at least two children are employed.

In Germany, a private foundation is making headway in attracting and retaining women in science and engineering. Led by physiologist and Nobel Prize winner Christiane Nüsslein-Volhard, the foundation awards grants to young female scientists to pay for baby-sitters and household help. "We lose talented women at the time they get pregnant . . . Later, these young women find it difficult to get back. They drop out," she said in an interview with the *New York Times*.[3] "We try to find the gifted ones, where it would be a real pity if they dropped out. We say, 'use these funds to buy yourself time away from household matters.'"[4]

These innovations show that change is possible when countries, foundations, and workplaces have the vision and commitment to see them through. While the problem seems complex, just a few simple institutional solutions could address many of the work–family conflicts parents currently face. As this book has shown, successful solutions must recognize that work–family choices occur across the entire life span beginning in the student years. The five transformative solutions suggested here will require, beyond putting new policies on the books, a commitment to change the culture at each step of the career path, with particular attention to the make-or-break years when women are most likely to drop down or drop out.

1. BREAK THE MAKE-OR-BREAK YEARS

All of our high-status professions are front-ended—the greatest demands are made on thirty- to forty-year-olds during the make-or-break decade. We need to rethink this century-old concept for the twenty-first century. The ideal workplace for the make-or-break years would start with a commitment to flexibility at the front end of a career—the years of greatest demand that collide with the childbearing years. Flexibility would take different forms across the professions but all would allow periods of less intense work followed by the right to return to the main track. In law it could be a part-time partnership track that allows the parent to take up to ten years (or more in special circumstances) before being considered for full partnership.

Most large law firms already offer a track of this kind, instituted during the first push for family-friendly policies in the 1980s, but it is rarely utilized. As senior partner Jessica Pers (whom we met in Chapter 4) noted, these are "graveyard" positions guaranteed to marginalize an employee and keep her from the best cases and the most powerful clients. These options have failed because the culture works against them and almost no men take the option. As Rena, the third-year law student introduced earlier, commented, "[All law students] know that daddy lawyers are partners, mommy lawyers are not."

But what if the senior partners introduced this option when they hired new employees, clearly set up the rules to make it workable, and backed it up with mentoring and resources, such as child care support, to make it work? What if men as well as women were seriously encouraged to take advantage of parental leave and flexible time, setting a new cultural norm for law practice?

Recently I met a successful corporate lawyer and mother of two children who reported that the part-time track at her firm was well utilized and well regarded. The secret, she said, is having part-timers available when the client needs service, even if it is their day off. "Your client doesn't know if you are full- or part-time; he doesn't see you everyday. Just as long as you are there when he needs you, all is well," she explained.

Her experience suggests that incorporating children into the fast track, especially during the crucial make-or-break years, may be possible in law if part-time attorneys operate under the principle that clients are always attended to, if not always at work.

Reformers are unanimous that firms must begin to conduct formal and informal surveys on the effectiveness of alternative work arrangements.[5] Joan Williams and Cynthia Calvert's 2001 Project for Attorney Retention suggests that firms should begin to measure comparative promotion rates between men and women.[6] Since one of the factors contributing to the low proportion of women partners is the practice of taking part-time attorneys off the partnership track, firms could test the accuracy of the perception that this practice ends all hope of promotion. Firms might also compare the attrition rates of attorneys on balanced schedules with those of attorneys on standard schedules. If the attrition rate among attorneys working reduced hours is higher than for other groups, there may be problems with existing "balanced hours" policies.[7]

The accounting firm Deloitte & Touche recognized in the early 1990s that women were rapidly leaking out the partnership pipeline. They considered this a bad business result and put in place practices that encouraged women to stay with the firm. These practices extended to their corporate law department, which is composed of 40 percent women employees. Attrition now is very low. While attorneys work forty- to fifty-hour weeks, their schedules are flexible, and they do not always have to put in face time at the office when working at home is a viable option.[8] Partnership decisions are carefully monitored to ensure that gender equality is maintained.

Deloitte & Touche has the numbers to prove that their policies make good business sense. A loyal, stable workforce is more productive than a revolving door. Other corporations, such as Citicorp, American Express, Ernst & Young, and Pfizer, have adopted more flexible work options for their workers, and all have seen improvement in employee retention. Pfizer has held on to its working mother employees by offering a three-day workweek option with the ability to return to full-time at any point.[9]

Genentech has taken this challenge a step further—the company not only accommodates working parents but celebrates them. The biotech company gives expectant moms a new-baby kit (complete with bib and pregnancy books) and a fully paid six-week leave after the baby is born. In addition, it has built twelve lactation rooms at four sites for nursing mothers. All employees at the company's headquarters in South San Francisco have access to an on-site child care center with full-time, backup, summer, and holiday care.

For computer powerhouse Hewlett-Packard, employee work–life issues became a top priority when former CEO Lew Platt lost his wife to cancer and found himself alone with two young children. Suddenly Platt discovered that flexible work–life balance was not a women's issue but a parents' issue. Today Hewlett-Packard encourages flexible work hours, job sharing, and telecommuting. According to Platt, these policies are the key to retaining talented employees in a competitive business.

These businesses have shown that flexible schedules are not only possible but practical. It's time for other fields to learn from their lesson.

2. CREATE SECOND CHANCES

Men and women who drop into the second tier or drop out of the professional world for a period of years must have opportunities to reenter the fast track—second chances to realize the professional goals they set out to achieve as ambitious young students. Parents need help in returning to the workforce after a long or short hiatus. Reentry training programs, networking resources, and temporarily reduced-hour jobs that offer phased-in full-time schedules are promising examples of progressive reentry policies.

Discounting the résumé gap would be a big step toward offering a second chance. In science and engineering fields, grants and fellowships routinely specify a limit to the number of years spent post-Ph.D. for an applicant, excluding those who have taken time out for family. Employers also follow this line of thought when hiring. Any applicant who has been off the fast track— even for a year or two—may not receive serious consideration. The federal government could change the rules governing these competitive grants (and all other federal employment for that matter) in a single swoop of family-friendly legislation that effectively creates second chances for academic parents. This legislation could also include grant supplements to pay for childbirth leave and one-year reentry postdoctoral fellowships that would allow parents an opportunity to ramp up to speed, even in highly competitive areas of science.

Business schools such as the Tuck School at Dartmouth and Babson College in Massachusetts have begun offering executive training programs for women executives seeking to return to the workforce. Some law schools, such as the Hastings College of the Law in San Francisco, are also considering reentry training programs for women that help "second-tiered" moms get back on the fast track. These programs are important steps in the right direction.

3. SUPPORT FAMILY AT ALL AGES

Family pressures are not limited to the make-or-break years. Becoming a parent can be the right choice for students in their twenties or early thirties—if universities and professional schools transform their chilly attitude into a warm welcome. The progress that Berkeley and other universities have made in providing child support, housing, paid leaves for working students, and a flexible curriculum are important new steps in keeping and retaining the next generation of talent.

Becoming a parent could also be right for women and men in their forties or fifties who choose to adopt. Of course children's needs do not stop at birth. Children can get sick at any time, and partners and parents can require immediate and extended care. The model of the Family Medical Leave Act (twelve weeks for any family-related illness) is a good one, but it needs to be completed with pay. Flexible part-time options will find the greatest support and acceptance if they are offered for all ages. In our survey of all UC faculty we found that the majority of men supported a part-time flexible track, especially if it could be taken at any time during the career. Women were enthusiastic about this possibility at any time, but especially during the make-or-break years.

4. ENCOURAGE FATHERS

As noted above, parental leave and reduced hours to care for young children should be routine for fathers as well as mothers. This would encourage stronger families and ensure that a flexible career pattern is not only a mommy track. Without fathers' participation, it is difficult to change the culture, and "family friendly" will come to mean "mommy trap." In Sweden, the government changed its generous eighteen-month parental leave policy to insist that fathers take at least six months of the total; otherwise the leave will be reduced to twelve months. The intention was not to save money but to make fatherly participation in raising children an accepted norm. In the university world fathers who provide substantial child care are now beginning routinely to stop their own tenure clock for childbirth. As this becomes the norm, the culture will no longer look on parental rights as women's rights.

5. IMPROVE THE SECOND TIER

The robust second tier, which has developed in all professions as a highly trained female labor force, is not likely to disappear. But it could be improved to ensure better conditions as well as opportunities back to a faster track. This would make it attractive to men as well women. In academia, reentry grants— whether federally subsidized or private—could help scholars bridge the gap between the world of the gypsy scholar and the demanding lead-up to tenure during the make-or-break years. Those who prefer the schedule and lifestyle that the second tier affords should be given job security, benefits, and pay that better represents their training and contribution. HMOs in the medical world provide a reasonable model for a functioning part-time second tier that is attractive to men as well as women. HMOs like Kaiser Permanente in California, while not competing with the scientific glamour of university research hospitals, offer good pay, security, and flexible schedules.

The final two suggestions are well-known and have been the subject of public debate for decades; nevertheless, little progress has been made. In fact, parental leave and child care seem to have fallen off the political agenda in the past few years. Where are the candidates who pledge to help working parents with the everyday support they need? Where are the voters who are demanding it?

All political candidates should be rated on their support of working families. At the top of the list should be the following:

Political support of parental leave. Policies that facilitate time off for and reentry after maternal or paternal leave are sorely needed, and the government should take the lead. Of the world's most developed industrial countries, only the United States and Australia do not offer government-mandated paid maternity leave.[10] Italy guarantees mothers a five-month maternity leave paid at 80 percent of the mother's wage, and both parents can take ten-month leaves at 30 percent of their earnings until the child's eighth birthday.[11] Notably, Italy, France, and Sweden offer time off to fathers as well as mothers. In contrast, the U.S. Family Leave Act gives new mothers just twelve weeks of *unpaid* leave after childbirth.

Child care that is high quality, flexible, and affordable is the cornerstone for all family-friendly policies in Europe as it must be in this country. Child care always tops the list of requests for family-friendly reforms. The greatest single boost to morale for parents at our university is the long-awaited opening of a new infant and toddler facility at the edge of campus. For students there will be subsidies, and for lower-income staff and faculty there will be scholarships. The companies with the greatest success in hiring and retaining parents make this a top priority. This should be a government priority as well.

PERSONAL STRATEGIES FOR SUCCESS

Institutional and legislative solutions are only part of the answer. As the women profiled in this book will attest, barriers to success exist not only in the workplace but also in the home. Societal stereotypes and expectations about parenting and gender play a role too. Solutions to the problem, I believe, are both personal and political.

Fortunately we now know better how mothers can plan their lives to succeed in spite of these of obstacles. The mothers in this book provide practical, personal guidelines that hold true across professions and generations. They also exhibit certainty that it can be done. They act with confidence and energy, often in the face of great resistance.

STAY IN THE GAME

Nearly all of the successful mothers interviewed in this book took little or no time off when their children were born. They did not believe they had the option to do so and still succeed—and they were probably right. Although 93 percent of highly qualified women want to return to work after taking time off in a study of corporate women, only 40 percent successfully return to full-time jobs.[12] And on average, these women lost 18 percent of their earning power when they returned to work after taking a break.[13]

Mothers who rose to the top of their professions worked reduced schedules for a while, but as psychiatry professor Lynn Pontin related, most returned to their jobs as soon as possible, and some even brought their children to work with them in order to do so. Our research shows that mothers who have children while in graduate school and persevere without taking years out do well. In the academic world, continuing to publish, even when not fully employed, can make the difference between a permanent second tier and a second chance. Until second chances become routine institutional practice, staying close to the center of action is critical.

Breaking the punitive cycle of the make-or-break years will allow more mothers to stay in the game as our successful mothers did. The strategies described above will give the mothers a break without terminating their career plans.

CHOOSE A GOOD PARTNER

Partners play a critical role for working mothers, but that role can be enabling or disabling. It is not a coincidence that most of the successful mothers interviewed attribute much of their accomplishment to their partners. Sometimes, as in the case of Senator Dianne Feinstein, the partner provides economic and emotional support. Other times, as in the case of Supreme Court Justice Ginsburg, the partner insists that the mother's career is equally important. Occasionally, as in the case of lawyer Carole C.'s husband, male partners break with gender stereotypes and stay at home with young children.

But many of the women we interviewed believed that partners constrained their careers. In two-career couples women often defer to their husband's job offer, as I did early in my career. Judith Kliman, the distinguished member of the National Academy of Sciences who appears in Chapter 6, related that following a divorce she had the freedom to advance her career by moving to a different university. And not all fathers believe that mothers should have a powerful, independent career. As one of our mothers sagely advised, "Don't marry a jerk."

An intriguing finding from our research is that single mothers do a little better than married mothers in achieving tenure.[14] When I ask the audience what their theory is, since our data do not offer explanations, I hear such answers as "They have no choice," to "They have fewer children to take care of."

LEARN MOTHER TIME

Successful fast track mothers learn how to adapt their schedules to what I call "mother time." They must firmly negotiate reduced hours for childbirth and other family needs. And they must say no to many late meetings and some business travel. Learning to negotiate a flexible schedule without becoming marginalized is a skill some possess naturally and others can learn. Basic classes in negotiation and time management are useful if mentors are not available. "Mother time" also means making the workplace work for you. As lawyer Jessica Pers commented, "My clients don't know if I am writing a brief from my office or from home." In other words, successful mothers are skilled tacticians who know when they must put in face time at the office and when it's okay to keep a less rigid schedule.

MIND YOUR MENTOR

As we've noted throughout this book, women on the fast track need guidance, and mentors are important at all career stages. The mothers we interviewed reported that mentors in graduate and professional schools greatly influenced their career direction. Some mentors, like my history professor, open the imagination or even the doors to the next important step. All along a career path, a mentor can make the difference between staying the course and dropping out, as did the encouragement of an older senior partner for Maryellen Herringer, the first woman in her law firm, when her clients treated her as an oddity, "like a talking dog." Mentoring is most critical during the student and make-or-break years, when women need the most help juggling career ambitions with family needs.

Mentors are not easy to find, in part because it is not usually in anyone's job description. As women rise in their careers they must make sure they bring younger women along with them and take responsibility for setting up a mentoring program in their workplace.

Mentoring about life issues should become routine in schools. Career/Life Planning 101 should be a part of every curriculum, beginning in high school and repeated in college. Forcing all young people to script out their adult lives—how they will organize their work and life and how they will achieve their ultimate goals—would assist them in planning a future in which they have real, not illusory, choices. During their graduate years, students should continue to be mentored not just for academic preparation but also for career/life preparation. Harvard University, for example, has offered a class for MBA students called Charting Your Course since 2001. It aims to help students factor in family issues to their long-range career plans. Special support is needed as students complete their training and face the job market—the danger zone period that triggers the exodus of women from the career pipeline. Women should be assisted in holding on to their professions and not veering into the second tier. Those who planned some part-time or time-out years for family would be encouraged to develop a life plan that included reentry.

Young women in science and engineering must receive special attention and encouragement from primary school onward. They should be recognized as a valuable, scarce resource in a country that is not producing enough trained technical minds to support our future growth and continued scientific innovation. NSF offers an Advance grant to universities that can offer innovative ways of advancing women through the competitive ranks of research science. Often a major component is an organized mentoring program. These grants have significantly changed the culture of participating universities.

TAKE A CHANCE ON SECOND CHANCES

Finally, successful fast track mothers take a gamble on a second chance. In our current workplace structure, there is little encouragement for mothers who leave their careers aside for a few years to return. But most mothers don't even try. Often they lose confidence and do not apply for positions or seek out old mentors for advice and direction. But second chance opportunities do arise, as they did for me. Maintaining contact with mentors and maintaining a foothold in the profession are the best ways to prepare for the opportunity.

MAKING IT HAPPEN

Recently my new colleague, the second woman dean to be appointed in five years, suggested we gather the handful of top-ranked women on campus to brainstorm about promoting women to leadership positions beyond the glass ceiling. We all knew that most women professors stalled at the associate professor level and felt worn out by the time they were full professors. Many turned down positions like department chair that would lead to higher authority and many were not asked. She said we already knew what it took to bring about change; we just needed to articulate the guidelines.

She was right. Over lunch we easily agreed on the following strategies, which could be a field manual for every CEO, law partner manager, chief of medicine, and editor in chief across the country.

- Take a chance on women who have not served as managers in line jobs such as department chairs, and advance them to a higher post. These women professors, particularly the mothers, have shown great drive, talent, and competence to get where they are, even if they have lost some time and not followed the traditional seniority sequence. Seniority, as measured by progressively responsible supervisory positions, is the usual criteria used for picking top leaders. Mothers who have deferred extra responsibilities in earlier years are often overlooked when they are ready to serve.

- Ensure that our loose association of faculty women, which already greets new women faculty and provides some guidance in the probationary years leading up to tenure, can continue to mentor beyond tenure. Commit senior women to becoming the cheerleaders for the next generation. Provide an "old girls' network" to match the advantage that "old boys" have usually given to young men.

  Such a support network is particularly needed to address the recruitment and retention of women in science. An informal group here at Berkeley, which also includes several prominent women scientists from UCSF, has been meeting bimonthly for almost thirty years. The group includes members elected to the National Academy of Sciences and the American Academy of Arts and Sciences, along with prestigious professorships and research positions. These high-achieving women all agree that continuous practical and emotional support is needed, and is a key to women's success in research and academic science.

- Encourage the chancellor and other top male executives to make appointing women leaders their own initiative. Convince them of the value of such appointments as a message to all young students that all doors are open to men and women equally. And on the business side of the house, point out they are taking advantage of some of the best and most capable talent in the university.

FINISHING

A revolution cannot be finished without continued passion. The revolutionary zeal of my generation has naturally expired. The days of public bra burning and man bashing, always a flashy sideshow to the main work of establishing equal footing in the workplace and in the law, is a memory, one that's sometimes embarrassing to the second generation. Their need to separate themselves from the *F* word, feminism, is understandable.

But the revolution was always for our daughters and now they must complete the task. The pioneer generation is beginning to retire. Young women, those who entered the workplace in the 1990s and early 2000s, and current students feel entitled to equal treatment but are unclear how to chart their own work and family life plans.

These generations must enlist the support of young men to succeed. Young men say they want a more balanced life, but will they actually pursue the changes that make it possible? Will they insist on a flexible workplace and then take their turn at parental leave? Will they encourage women to continue their careers on an equal footing to the very top positions? Improving work–life policies for men must be a key element of any solution. A Center for Work–Life Policy study found that 48 percent of professional men feel that part-time options are perceived as illegitimate in their workplace culture, even when it's part of official policy. That culture needs to change before men are able to participate equally in family life with women.

There are hopeful signs that momentum exists to change the structure of the workplace, but will our daughters fight to see it through? We know they are less willing to give up family for work, but are they willing to change the workplace rather than retreat to the home? My generation, still keenly aware of our struggle to gain recognition as professionals, hopes that the answer is a resounding yes.

—Mary Ann Mason

Will my generation continue the struggle started by the pioneer generation, or will we retreat to the home? This is a timely question and one that's difficult to untangle in the current mixed-message environment. I believe we will continue to fight for more rights, but in our own way; we may not follow the exact path of our pioneer mothers.

When I began working on this project in early 2004, family and feminism were far from my mind. At twenty-four, I had just resigned from a job in the photography department of a prestigious men's fashion magazine in New York City and had moved back to San Francisco after six years in the Big Apple. I was enjoying the freedom of doing freelance writing and photography by day, and doing street outreach for a women's community clinic by night. Like many people my age I knew that family would probably be part of my future, but I hadn't given the idea deep thought. And I had not considered how my career would affect choices about family. This topic was as abstract as the 401k plan options I was supposed to choose from at my first full-time job with benefits.

Over the course of this project, however, my perspective changed. I discovered a new awareness of how work and family issues have played out historically and how they are currently influencing the lives of my peers as well as my own life. My mother's generation removed the barriers to career opportunity for my generation, but the pioneers still worked a second shift at home—their revolution fell short of achieving equality for women.

While my generation seems less interested in a highly public battle akin to the feminist movement of the 1960s (feminism and bra burning seem decidedly uncool), we are challenging stereotypes that enable gender inequality in the home. Women don't consider it a given that they will do the majority of housework and young men aren't opting out of caretaking responsibilities. Many young men want a more active role in parenting and are choosing less demanding careers in order to make that happen.

In my own class of recent professional school graduates, couples are approaching work–life issues with equality in mind. I recently met a fellow classmate from my social work program to celebrate our graduation and discuss our future professional plans. She and her husband of two years have been discussing children seriously in the past six months and she felt compelled to take a job she felt would accommodate family. But importantly, her husband also considered family obligations. His job allows a flexible schedule and he has told her he will be happy to accommodate whatever her schedule is. It's a heartening development that many young couples today are approaching this issue on equal footing. Neither one assumes that the woman will take on all of the care duties.

This approach stems in part from our experiences growing up in split family households. At least half of my friends had divorced parents. They shuttled back and forth between parents and witnessed some of the difficulty, if not animosity, of these breakups. The result of this awareness probably undermines my generation's faith in marriage, but it also inspires a healthier approach to the institution, and a more practical attitude about career–life issues. We don't assume that married couples live happily ever after. Success requires negotiation and communication at every step of the way.

In the burgeoning days of the feminist movement an unfortunate decision to demonize and blame men for the unequal status of women polarized many male supporters of women's equality. As a correction, it is especially important to include men in the discussions and plans for solutions.

Female identity and responsibilities are in a state of flux and almost caught between epochs—the Donna Reed happy homemaker and some unclear vision of an equal self-actualized woman of the future (which I hope is not exemplified by the superficial, self-absorbed characters in *Sex in the City*). As a child I watched the programs of the great animators Bill Hanna and Joe Barbera, who created all sorts of clever spacescapes and timesaving technologies for the Jetsons' futurized life. But they made sure the mother, Jane Jetson, was busy selecting dinner from the machine screen, taking care of the kids' cyber toys, and organizing the home with the help of Rosey, the robo-maid. George Jetson sped off in his little spacecraft to work each day. The women of my generation need to challenge this vision, and changing the paradigm requires a new consciousness from both men and women. Balancing work and child rearing is a family issue, not a mother issue.

The pressure to be a certain kind of mother—one who sacrifices career for children—exists even today with the resurgence of the new momism movement. Looking back, I realize that my mother—like many successful women in this book—was able to rise above the social pressure to conform to a certain maternal stereotype. I grew up with full-time working parents, but I never felt that I was shortchanged on maternal or paternal time. In fact the role my mother modeled for me was one of being ambitious and loving; I saw no contradiction there. Her choices factored directly into my own drive and ambitions.

But my mom would sometimes question her path. She would joke about not being the "Donna Reed mom," buying cupcakes at the store instead of baking cookies. My first semester in college my dorm roommate's mother was endlessly sending her baked goods and other personalized goodies and presents; she was a stay-at-home mother and my roommate was her only child. I remember my mom calling while my roommate was opening one of these packages. She lamented that she had been swamped with her teaching schedule and had not been able to do something like that for me. A week later I received a package. She had ordered an enormous cheese wheel online and had it sent to my room. It didn't matter that my mother had a successful career and two well-adjusted children; self-doubt still crept in now and again. I realize now that letting go of this mother guilt and charting your own path requires independence, self-confidence, and sacrifice.

To my surprise, some of the graduate students I interviewed made me realize that there are also advantages to having children while still an apprentice. As a graduate student I never considered that my schedule would be well suited for starting a family. However, after hearing about the long hours required for most first positions, from lawyers to lecturers, I revisited this notion. For most graduate students, children and family fall farther down the to-do list; cultivating career and establishing work stability often trump these urges and desires. For most professional women having a child without job security seems risky and difficult. However, the risks and difficulties of having children later on are also significant. I was warned by a number of women who waited to have children that, though there appears to be infinite choice in family planning with modern contraception and fertilization techniques, there is still significant difficulty, if not failure, when trying to conceive later in the reproductive years.

The women in this book, like my mother, taught me many important life lessons. Some of the best family planning advice I have heard came from Ashley Dunning, a powerful young San Francisco lawyer currently planning her family with concise attention. She described the importance of knowing your worth. A lack of confidence and perceived workplace productivity requirements, more than the actual demands of the firm, is what leads many women to make time commitments that overextend their capabilities. Confidence in career comes with stability according to Ashley; some women find stability from spouses, real work experience, or advanced degrees. All can contribute to building a firm platform to solidly stand on.

Although a number of interviewees identified the importance of time set aside for themselves, others found being with their children more fulfilling than time spent any other way. Clearly there are differences in styles among all mothers, even fast track mothers. The pace and schedule of many of the women I interviewed could seem unappealing to some and exciting to others, just as some women love the infancy stage and others prefer toddlers or later years. Women will find ways to have children, and some will find that balance with career ambitions. The goal is for women to have more choices: to stay home, keep working, move up and on, and have more children.

I hope these lessons—and the other important issues raised in this book— serve as a piece of an ongoing dialog about women, family, and work. We will need continuous discussion, research, and thought to move toward the kind of cultural, societal, and legislative changes necessary.

—Eve Mason Ekman

NOTES

INTRODUCTION
DO BABIES MATTER? MOTHERS ON THE FAST TRACK

1. National Center for Education Statistics, *IPEDS Salaries, Tenure, and Fringe Benefits of Full-Time Instructional Faculty Survey* (NCES, 2001).
2. Arlie Hochschild, *The Second Shift* (New York: Penguin, 2003).
3. Anne Crittenden, *The Price of Motherhood* (New York: Owl, 2002).
4. Joan Williams, *Unbending Gender* (New York: Oxford University Press, 2000).
5. Mary Ann Mason, *The Equality Trap* (New York: Simon & Schuster, 1988).
6. Mary Ann Mason and Marc Goulden, "Do Babies Matter? The Effect of Family Formation on the Lifelong Careers of Academic Men and Women," *Academe,* November–December 2002, pp. 21–27; Mason and Goulden, "Do Babies Matter (Part II): Closing the Baby Gap," *Academe* 90, no. 6 (2004): 3–7.
7. Ruth Rosen, *The World Split Open* (New York: Penguin, 2001). 91–92.

CHAPTER ONE
THE "MOTHER PROBLEM": UP, OUT, OR SIDELINED?

1. Jennifer Steinhauer, "For Women in Medicine, a Road to Compromise, Not Perks," *New York Times,* March 1, 1999.
2. Ann Boulis, "The Evolution of Gender and Motherhood in Contemporary Medicine," *Annals of the American Academy of Political and Social Science,* November 2004.
3. Association of American Medical Colleges, *U.S. Medical School Faculty Trends, 1995–2005,* www.aamc.org/data/facultyroster/reports.htm.
4. Eliot Marshall, "Science Notes," *Science,* May 18, 2001, pp. 1288–1289.
5. National Center for Education Statistics, *Research and Development Report August 2000: Entry and Persistence of Women and Minorities in College Science and Engineering Education* (NCES, 2001), p. 22.
6. Steinhauer, "Women in Medicine."
7. National Center for Education Statistics, *First Professional Degrees Conferred by Degree-Granting Institutions, by Racial/Ethnic Group and Sex of Student: Se-*

lected Years, 1976–77 to 2001–02, http://nces.ed.gov/programs/digest/d03/tables/dt273.asp.

8. *Vital Statistics of the United States: Natality 1970: Births: Final Data for 2000* (NCHS, 2002).

9. U.S. Census Bureau, *Public Use Microdata Sample (PUMS)*, 2003.

10. Mary Ann Mason, Angelica Stacy, and Marc Goulden, *The UC Faculty Work and Family Survey*, 2003, http://ucfamilyedge.berkeley.edu.

11. V. L. Seltzer, "Changes and Challenges for Women in Academic Obstetrics and Gynecology," *American Journal of Obstetrics and Gynecology* 180 (1999): 837–848.

12. U.S. Census Bureau, *Public Use Microdata Sample (PUMS)*, 2003.

13. Timothy L. O'Brien, "Up the Down Staircase: Why Do So Few Women Reach the Top of Big Law Firms?" *New York Times*, March 19, 2006, sec. 3, p. 4.

14. Sue Shellenberger, "The Mommy Drain: Employers Beef Up Perks to Lure New Mothers Back to Work," *Wall Street Journal*, September 28, 2006, Personal Journal, p. 1.

CHAPTER TWO
THE STUDENT YEARS: EIGHTEEN TO THIRTY-TWO

1. *Digest of Education Statistics* (National Center for Education Statistics, 2001).

2. *Digest of Education Statistics* (National Center for Education Statistics, 2000).

3. *Digest of Education Statistics* (National Center for Education Statistics, 2000).

4. Michele Patterson and Laurie Engelberg, "Women in Male-Dominated Professions," in Ann Stromberg and Shirley Harkess, eds., *Women Working* (Palo Alto, CA: Mayfield, 1978), 270.

5. Commission on Professionals in Science and Technology, "What Does the Future of the Science Labor Market Look Like?" www.cpst.org.

6. Elga Wasserman, *The Door and the Dream: Conversations with Eminent Women in Science* (Washington, D.C.: Joseph Henry, 2000), p. 26.

7. J. Scott Long, ed., *From Scarcity to Visibility: Gender Differences in the Careers of Doctoral Scientists and Engineers* (Washington, D.C.: National Academies Press, 2001).

8. Claudia Dreifus, "The Chilling of American Science," *New York Times*, July 6, 2004, p. D2.

9. Thomas Hoffer et al., *Doctorate Recipients from United States Universities: Summary Report* (Chicago: NORC, 2005).

10. *Vital Statistics of the United States: Natality 1970* (National Center for Health Statistics, 2002), Births: Final Data for 2000.

11. Mary Ann Mason and Marc Goulden, "Babies Matter: Pushing the Gender Equity Revolution Forward," in *Enhancing Understanding of Faculty Roles and Worklives*, ed. S. Bracken et al. (Sterling, VA: Stylus, 2006), p. 6.

12. *Vital Statistics of the United States: Natality 1970* (National Center for Health Statistics, 2002), Births: Final Data for 2000.

13. *UC Berkeley Graduate Student Housing Survey,* 2001.

14. American Women's Medical Association, *Position Paper on Maternity Leave During Training,* November 1996, www.jamwa.org.

15. Robin Wilson, "The Law of Physics: A Postdoc's Pregnancy Derails Her Career," *Chronicle of Higher Education* 52, no. 12 (2006): A10.

16. Maresi Nerad, Joe Cerny, and Linda McPheron, *UC Berkeley and LBNL Postdoc Survey,* 1999.

17. Mary Ann Mason and Marc Goulden, "Do Babies Matter? The Effect of Family Formation on the Lifelong Careers of Academic Men and Women," *Academe,* November–December 2002, pp. 21–27.

18. Mason and Goulden, "Do Babies Matter?"

19. Mason and Goulden, "Do Babies Matter?"

20. Preliminary results based on survival analysis of the *Survey of Doctorate Recipients,* a national biennial longitudinal data set funded by the National Science Foundation and others, 1979 to 1995. Percentages take into account discipline, age, ethnicity, Ph.D. calendar year, time to Ph.D. degree, and National Research Council academic reputation rankings of Ph.D. program effects. For each event (Ph.D. to TT job procurement, or associate to full professor), data is limited to a maximum of sixteen years. The waterline is an artistic rendering of the statistical effects of family and gender.

21. Nicholas H. Wolfinger, Mary Ann Mason, and Marc Goulden, "Problems in the Pipeline: Gender, Marriage, and Fertility in the Ivory Tower" (paper presented at the annual meeting of the American Sociological Association, San Francisco, 2004).

22. Wasserman, *The Door and the Dream,* p. 17.

23. ABA Commission on Women, *The Unfinished Agenda: A Report on the Status of Women in the Legal Profession,* www.abanet.org/ftp/pub/women/unfinished agenda.pdf; American Medical Association, *Physician Characteristics and Distribution in the U.S.,* 2005 edition and earlier editions, www.ama-assn.org/ama/pub/category/12912.html.

24. Yilu Zhao, "Beyond Sweetie," *New York Times,* November 7, 2004, Education Life sec., p. 20.

25. Wolfinger, Mason, and Goulden, "Problems in the Pipeline."

CHAPTER THREE
THE MAKE-OR-BREAK YEARS: THIRTY TO FORTY

1. Annenberg Public Policy Center, *The Glass Ceiling Persists: The Third Annual APPC Report on Women Leaders in Communication Companies,* 2003, p. 12, appcpenn.org.

2. Deborah L. Rhode, *Unfinished Agenda: Women and the Legal Profession,* ABA Report, 2001, p. 14.

3. *Hishon v. King and Spalding* (No. 82-940), Supreme Court Collection, Cornell University Law School, http://supct.law.cornell.edu/supct/html/historics/USSC_CR_0467_0069_ZS.html.

4. Women's Bar Association of Massachusetts, *More Than Part Time: The Effect of Reduced Hours Arrangements on the Retention, Recruitment, and Success of Women Attorneys in Law Firms,* 2000, p. 16, http://womenlaw.stanford.edu/mass.rpt.html.

5. Jerry A. Jacobs and Kathleen Gerson, *The Time Divide: Work, Family, and Gender Inequality* (Cambridge: Harvard University Press, 2005), p. 35.

6. Rhode, *Unfinished Agenda.*

7. *Women and Attorneys of Color at Law Firms,* 2002, p. 14, www.nalp.org/nalp research/mw02sum.htm; Rhode, *Unfinished Agenda.*

8. Rhode, *Unfinished Agenda,* p. 14.

9. Boston Bar Association Task Force on Professional Challenges and Family Needs, *Facing the Grail: Confronting the Cost of Work-Family Imbalance,* 1999.

10. NALP Foundation, *Associate Attrition Rates Changed Minimally since 1997,* www .nalp.org/press/bidwars.htm.

11. Deborah L. Rhode, *Balanced Lives: Changing the Culture of the Legal Profession,* 2001, www.abanet.org/women/glance.pdf.

12. Mary Ann Mason and Marc Goulden, "Marriage and Baby Blues: Redefining Gender Equity in the Academy," *Annals of the American Academy of Political and Social Science,* November 2004, p. 98.

13. Lisa Belkin, "Effects Are Unclear of Limits on Medical Residents' Health," *New York Times,* February 2, 1995.

14. Lawrence K. Altman and Denise Goody, "Hospital Accreditation Will Strictly Limit Hours of Residents," *New York Times,* June 14, 2002.

15. AMWA, *Balancing Life/Family,* 2000, http://students.amwa-doc.org/resources/index.htm; "Woman Physician in the Year 2000," *JAMWA* 55, no. 1 (2000); AMA Statistics, Women Medical School Applicants 2002; Kellogg Foundation Study, 19.

16. American Medical Association. Updated 1997, AMA Chicago, 1998.

17. Ann Boulis, "The Evolution of Gender and Motherhood," *Annals of the American Academy of Political and Social Science,* November 4, 2004, p. 196.

18. www.aamc.org/members/wim/statistics/stats03/table3.pdf

19. Association of American Medical Colleges, *Women in U.S. Academic Medicine 2002–2003,* www.aamc.org/members/wim/statistics/stats03/start.htm.

20. J. Bickel, K. Croft, and R. Marshall, *Enhancing the Environment for Women in Academic Medicine* (Washington, D.C.: AAMC, 1996).

21. Association of American Medical Colleges, *Women in U.S. Academic Medicine Statistics, 1999–2000* (Washington, D.C.: AAMC, 2001).

22. *Science Policy: On the Physician Supply Debate,* http://scienceweek.com/2004/sb040827-3.htm.

23. Boulis, "Evolution of Gender and Motherhood," pp. 20–35.

24. National Science Foundation, *Science and Engineering Indicators 2004,* www.nsf.gov/statistics/seind04/c3/c3s2.htm.

25. Mason and Goulden, "Marriage and Baby Blues," p. 97.

26. Mason and Goulden, "Marriage and Baby Blues," p. 93.

27. Mason and Goulden, "Marriage and Baby Blues," p. 98.

28. Mary Ann Mason and Marc Goulden, "Do Babies Matter (Part II): Closing the Baby Gap," *Academe* 90, no. 6 (2004): 3.

29. Annenberg Public Policy Center, *The Glass Ceiling Persists: The Third Annual APPC Report on Women Leaders in Communication Companies,* 2003, pp. 35–36, appcpenn.org.

30. Annenberg Public Policy Center, *Glass Ceiling,* p. 12.

31. Annenberg Public Policy Center, *Glass Ceiling,* p. 12.

32. Sheila Wellington, Marcia Brumit Kropf, and Paulette Gerkovich, "What's Holding Women Back?" *Harvard Business Review* 81 (2003): 18–19.

33. Graduate Management Admission Council, www.gmac.com/gmac/NewsCenter/PressReleases/SalariesforNewMBAsTop92000.htm.

34. Aspen Institute Business and Society, *Where Will They Lead?* Program Study 2003, www.aspeninstitute.org/atf/cf/{DEB6F227-659B-4EC8-8F84-8DF23CA704F5}/SAS.pdf.

35. Gregg Schoenfeld, *Work–Life Balance: An MBA Alumni Report,* Graduate Management Admission Council Research Report RR-05-09, October 13, 2005.

36. Schoenfeld, *Work–Life Balance.*

37. Rose Mary Wentling, "The Career Development and Aspirations of Women in Middle Management—Revisited," *Women in Management Review* 18, no. 5–6 (2003): 311–324.

38. Patrick McGeehan, "Panel Finds Bias Against Women at Merrill Lynch," *New York Times,* Wednesday, April 21, 2004, p. 1.

39. Catherine Kirchmeyer, "Gender Differences in Managerial Careers: Yesterday, Today, and Tomorrow," *Journal of Business Ethics* 37 (2002): 5–24.

40. PARS, *Better on Balance? The Corporate Counsel Work/Life Report,* December 2003, p. 24.

41. "Deloitte Recognized by City of New York As One of the Five Best Employers in New York City for Women," October 2003, www.deloitte.com/dtt/press_release/0,2309,sid percent253D2283 percent2526cid percent253D28320,00.html.

42. Mason and Goulden, "Do Babies Matter (Part II)."

43. U.S. Census Bureau, *Public Use Microdata Sample (PUMS)*, 2003.

44. U.S. Census Bureau, *Public Use Microdata Sample*.

45. Mason and Goulden, "Marriage and Baby Blues," pp. 86–103.

46. Ellen Galinsky et al., *Leaders in a Global Economy: A Study of Executive Women and Men*, www.catalystwomen.org.

47. U.S. Census Bureau, *Public Use Microdata Sample*.

48. AMWA, *Position Paper on Pregnancy During Schooling, Training, and Early Practice Years*, 1993, www.amwa-doc.org/publications/Position_Papers/pregnancy htm.htm.

49. U.S. Census Bureau, *Public Use Microdata Sample*.

50. "Graduate Medical Education," *JAMA* 290 (2003): 1234–1248.

51. AMWA, *Position Paper on Maternity Leave During Training*, November 1996, www.jamwa.org.

CHAPTER FOUR
MOTHERS' CHOICES: STAYING THE COURSE, OPTING OUT,
OR DROPPING DOWN

1. National Public Radio, *Only in America: An Interview with Justice Ruth Bader Ginsburg*, January 6, 1995.

2. Claudia Goldin, "The Long Road to the Fast Track: Career and Family," *Annals of the American Academy of Political and Social Science* 596, no. 1 (2004): 20–35.

3. Goldin, "Long Road to the Fast Track," p. 23.

4. Goldin, "Long Road to the Fast Track," p. 23.

5. Goldin, "Long Road to the Fast Track," p. 23.

6. Goldin, "Long Road to the Fast Track," p. 23.

7. Carolyn Teich Adams and Kathryn Teich Winston, *Mothers at Work: Public Policies in the United States, Sweden, and China* (New York: Longman, 1980), p. 66.

8. Laraine T. Zappert, *Getting It Right: How Working Mothers Successfully Take Up the Challenge of Life, Family, and Career* (New York: Simon & Schuster, 2002).

9. Zappert, *Getting It Right*, p. 123.

10. Mary Ann Mason and Marc Goulden, "Do Babies Matter? The Effect of Family Formation on the Lifelong Careers of Academic Men and Women," *Academe*, November–December 2002, pp. 21–27.

11. Ann Boulis, "The Evolution of Gender and Motherhood in Contemporary Medicine," *Annals of the American Academy of Political and Social Science*, November 2004, p. 177.

12. Mary Ann Mason and Marc Goulden, "Marriage and Baby Blues: Redefining Gender Equity in the Academy," *Annals of the American Academy of Political and Social Science,* November 2004, pp. 86–103.

13. Mary Blair-Loy and Amy S. Wharton, "Mothers in Finance: Surviving and Thriving," *Annals of the American Academy of Political and Social Science,* November 2004.

14. Mary C. Noonan and Mary E. Corcoran, "The Mommy Track and Partnership: Temporary Delay or Dead End?" *Annals of the American Academy of Political and Social Science,* November 2004, pp. 130–151.

15. Mason and Goulden, "Do Babies Matter?" pp. 21–27.

16. C. H. Kinsley et al., "Motherhood Improves Learning and Memory," *Nature,* November 11, 1999.

17. U.S. Census Bureau, *Public Use Microdata Sample (PUMS),* 2003.

18. Lisa Belkin, "The Opt Out Revolution," *New York Times Magazine,* October 26, 2003.

19. U.S. Census Bureau, *Public Use Microdata Sample.*

20. Caitlin Flanagan, "To Hell with All That," *New Yorker,* July 2004, p. 40.

21. Susan J. Douglas and Meredith W. Michaels, *The Mommy Myth* (New York: Free Press, 2004), p. 6.

22. Jesse Bernard, *The Future of Motherhood* (New York: Dial, 1974), p. 42.

23. Margaret Mead, "Some Theoretical Consideration of the Problems of Mother-Child Separation," *American Journal of Orthopsychiatry* 24 (1954): 24.

24. Stephanie Armour, "Moms Find It Easier to Pop Back in Workforce," *USA Today,* September 23, 2004, Money sec.

25. Sylvia Ann Hewlett and Carolyn Buck Luce, "Off Ramps and On Ramps: Keeping Talented Women on the Road to Success," *Harvard Business Review* 9416 (2005).

26. Hewlett and Luce, "Off Ramps and On Ramps."

27. *University of California Faculty Family Friendly Edge: An Initiative for Tenure-Track Faculty at the University of California,* 2002, http://ucfamilyedge.berkeley.edu.

28. *University of California Faculty Family Friendly Edge.*

29. Armour, "Moms Find It Easier."

30. Sarah Hrdy, *Mother Nature* (New York: Pantheon, 1999), p. 139.

31. Hrdy, *Mother Nature,* p. 90.

32. *University of California Faculty Family Friendly Edge.*

33. Pamela Stone and Meg Lovejoy, "Fast-Track Women and the 'Choice' to Stay Home," *Annals of the American Academy of Political and Social Science,* November 2004, p. 68.

34. Stone and Lovejoy, "Fast-Track Women," p. 68.

35. Zappert, *Getting It Right,* p. 137.

CHAPTER FIVE
THE SECOND TIER

1. U.S. Department of Education/National Center for Education Statistics, *Fall Staff in Postsecondary Institutions, 1993* (Washington, D.C.: USDE, 1996), pp. 24–25. The two surveys in USDE/NCES, *1993 National Study of Postsecondary Faculty: Methodology Report* (Washington, D.C.: USDE, 1997) in fall 1992 found 42 and 43 percent.

2. Ann Boulis, "The Evolution of Gender and Motherhood in Contemporary Medicine," *Annals of the American Academy of Political and Social Science,* November 2004, p. 192.

3. A term coined by Joan Williams to describe the male workplace model. Joan Williams, *Unbending Gender* (New York: Oxford University Press, 2000).

4. Jennifer Steinhauer, "For Women in Medicine, a Road to Compromise, Not Perks," *New York Times,* March 1, 1999.

5. AMA Statistics, "Women Residents by Specialty, 2002," www.ama-assn.org/ama/pub/category/12915.html.

6. AMA Statistics, "Women Residents by Specialty, 2004," www.ama-assn.org/ama/pub/category/12915.html.

7. Boulis, "Evolution of Gender and Motherhood," p. 192.

8. Amy E. Wallace and William B. Weeks, "Differences in Income Between Male and Female Primary Care Physicians," *JAMWA,* November 4, 2002, pp. 180–184.

9. Boulis, "Evolution of Gender and Motherhood," p. 196.

10. Steinhauer, "For Women in Medicine, a Road to Compromise."

11. Steinhauer, "For Women in Medicine, a Road to Compromise."

12. U.S. Census Bureau, *Public Use Microdata Sample (PUMS),* 2003.

13. Del Jones, "Not So Good Year for Female CEOs," *USA Today,* December 22, 2005.

14. Center for Women's Business Research, "Completing the Picture: Equally Owned Firms," 2002, www.nfwbo.org/CompletingthePicture.htm.

15. "Why Companies Lose Female Talent and What They Can Do About It," *Women Entrepreneurs,* 9. *Catalyst Report* 2 (1998).

16. "Why Companies Lose Female Talent."

17. David Carr, "Accepting a Webby? Brevity, Please," *New York Times,* June 8, 2005, B1.

18. "The CEO Still Wears Wingtips: Jobs That Lead to the Top Remain Overwhelmingly Female-Free," *Business Week,* November 22, 1999, pp. 82–90.

19. Sheila Wellington, Marcia Brumit Kropf, and Paulette Gerkovich, "What's Holding Women Back?" *Harvard Business Review* 81 (2003): 18–19.

20. Mary C. Mattis, "Women Corporate Directors in the United States," in Ronald J. Burke and Mary C. Mattis, *Women on Corporate Boards of Directors: International Challenges and Opportunities* (Dordrecht: Kluwer, 2000), 43.

21. "CEO Still Wears Wingtips."

22. Mary C. Noonan and Mary E. Corcoran, "The Mommy Track and Partnership: Temporary Delay or Dead End?" *Annals of the American Academy of Political and Social Science,* November 1, 2004, 20–35.

23. Noonan and Corcoran, "Mommy Track and Partnership," 11.

24. Mary Ann Mason and Marc Goulden, "Do Babies Matter? The Effect of Family Formation on the Lifelong Careers of Academic Men and Women," *Academe,* November–December 2002; Laraine T. Zappert, *Getting It Right: How Working Mothers Successfully Take Up the Challenge of Life, Family, and Career* (New York: Simon & Schuster, 2002).

25. Deborah L. Rhode, "Balanced Lives: Changing the Culture of the Legal Profession," 2001, www.abqnet.org/women/glance.pdf.

26. "Balanced Lives," p. 16; NALP Research, Part Time Lawyers, 2001.

27. Joan Williams and Cynthia Calvert, *Balanced Hours: Effective Part-Time Policies for Washington Law Firms,* Project for Attorney Retention, August 2001, www.pardc.org.

28. Michael Goldhaber, "Part-Time Never Works," *National Law Journal,* December 2000.

29. Rhode, "Balanced Lives," p. 16.

30. Deborah Rhode, *Unfinished Agenda: Women and the Legal Profession,* ABA Report, 2001, p. 14.

31. "Balanced Lives," p. 37.

32. Chris Klein, "Women's Progress Slows at Top Firms," *National Law Journal,* May 6, 1996, p. A1.

33. Klein, "Women's Progress Slows."

34. More Than Part-Time, p. 60.

35. More Than Part-Time, p. 17.

36. National Association of Legal Professionals, *Jobs and J.D.s: Employment of New Law Graduates, Class of 2004,* NALP Report, www.nalp.org/nalpresearch/median02.htm.

37. NALP, *Jobs and J.D.s.*

38. PARS, *Better on Balance? The Corporate Counsel Work/Life Report,* December 2003, p. 3.

39. Mason and Goulden, "Do Babies Matter?" pp. 21–27.

40. *University of California Faculty Family Friendly Edge: An Initiative for Tenure-Track Faculty at the University of California,* 2002, http://ucfamilyedge.berkeley.edu.

41. For an account of this controversy, see Ann Crittenden, *The Price of Motherhood* (New York: Metropolitan, 2001), pp. 30–32.

42. Pamela Stone and Meg Lovejoy, "Fast-Track Women and the 'Choice' to Stay Home," *The Annals of the American Academy of Political and Social Science,* 11/2004; vol. 596: pp. 62–83.

43. Julia Overturf Johnson and Barbara Downs, *Maternity Leave and Employment Patterns of First Time Mothers: 1961–2000* (Washington, D.C.: U.S. Dept. of Commerce, 2005).

44. Boulis, "Evolution of Gender and Motherhood," p. 177.

CHAPTER SIX
BEYOND THE GLASS CEILING: FORTY TO SIXTY-FIVE AND BEYOND

1. "The Conundrum of the Glass Ceiling," *Economist*, July 21, 2005.

2. Mary C. Noonan and Mary E. Corcoran, "The Mommy Track and Partnership: Temporary Delay or Dead End?" *Annals of the American Academy of Political and Social Science*, November 2004, pp. 130–151.

3. Ann Boulis, "The Evolution of Gender and Motherhood in Contemporary Medicine," *Annals of the American Academy of Political and Social Science*, November 2004, pp. 172–206.

4. "Conundrum of the Glass Ceiling."

5. Deborah L. Rhode, *Unfinished Agenda: Women and the Legal Profession*, ABA Report, 2001, p. 14.

6. Donna Coffman, "Women Deans Optimistic About Increasing Their Numbers," *AAMC Reporter*, February 2005.

7. National Academy of Sciences Press Office interview, April 10, 2006.

8. Patrick McGeehan, "Panel Finds Bias Against Women at Merrill Lynch," *New York Times*, April 21, 2004, p. 1.

9. *Women in U.S. Corporate Leadership* (Catalyst, 2003).

10. *Price v. Waterhouse*, 490 U.S. 228; 109.

11. "Conundrum of the Glass Ceiling."

12. "Conundrum of the Glass Ceiling."

13. Ellen Galinsky et al., *Leaders in a Global Economy: A Study of Executive Women and Men* (Boston: Families and Work Institute, 2002); study commissioned by Catalyst).

14. Galinsky et al., *Leaders in a Global Economy.*

15. Galinsky et al., *Leaders in a Global Economy.*

16. "A Study on the Status of Women Faculty in Science at MIT," *MIT Faculty Newsletter*, March 1999.

17. Lisa Trie, "Biases Must Be Tackled to Achieve Gender Equity in Mathematics, Scholars Argue," *Stanford Report*, February 15, 2006.

18. National Science Foundation, Division of Science Resources Statistics, *Gender Differences in the Careers of Academic Scientists and Engineers: A Literature Review*, June 2003.

19. National Science Foundation, *Gender Differences.*

20. Trie, "Biases Must Be Tackled."

21. Virginia Valian, *Why So Slow: The Advancement of Women?* (Cambridge: MIT Press, 1998), p. 3.

22. *Women Entrepreneurs: Why Companies Lose Female Talent and What They Can Do About It* (New York: Catalyst, 1998); Mary Ann Mason and Marc Goulden, "Do Babies Matter? The Effect of Family Formation on the Lifelong Careers of Academic Men and Women," *Academe,* November–December 2002; Elga Wasserman, *The Door and the Dream: Conversations with Eminent Women in Science* (Washington, D.C.: Joseph Henry, 2000).

23. Sylvia Ann Hewlett and Carolyn Buck Luce, "Off Ramps and On Ramps: Keeping Talented Women on the Road to Success," *Harvard Business Review,* 2005.

24. U.S. Census Bureau, *Public Use Microdata Sample (PUMS),* 2003.

25. Catherine Kirchmeyer, "Gender Differences in Managerial Careers: Yesterday, Today, and Tomorrow," *Journal of Business Ethics* 37 (2002): 5–24.

26. Phyllis L. Carr, Janet Bickel, and Thomas S. Inui, eds., *Taking Root in a Forest Clearing: A Resource Guide for Medical Faculty* (Kellogg Foundation, n.d.), p. 58.

27. Hewlett and Luce, "Off Ramps and On Ramps."

28. Wasserman, *The Door in the Dream,* p. 191.

29. Wasserman, *The Door in the Dream,* p. 177.

30. National Academy of Sciences Press Office interview, April 10, 2006.

31. *Disability and Retirement: The Early Exit of Baby Boomers from the Labor Force,* Congressional Budget Office Report, November 2004, www.cbo.gov/ftpdocs/60xx/doc6018/11-22-LaborForce.pdf.

32. Sharon Linstedt, "Lawsuit Puts Spotlight on Caregiver Discrimination," *Buffalo News,* June 7, 2004, B6.

33. Sloan Work and Family Research Network, "Number of Caregiver Discrimination Cases, 1970–2005," *Network News,* April 2005.

34. For a full discussion of maternal discrimination, see Joan Williams and Nancy Segal, "Beyond the Maternal Wall: Relief for Family Caregivers Who Are Discriminated Against on the Job," *Harvard Women's Law Journal* 26 (2003): 77.

35. Williams and Segal, "Beyond the Maternal Wall, pp. 77, 95.

36. Williams and Segal, "Beyond the Maternal Wall, p. 96.

37. Williams and Segal, "Beyond the Maternal Wall, p. 127.

38. Timothy L. O'Brien, "Up the Down Staircase: Why Do So Few Women Reach the Top of Big Law Firms?" *New York Times,* March 1, 2006, sec. 3, p. 1.

39. U.S. Equal Employment Opportunity Commission, *Diversity in Law Firms 2003,* www.eeoc.gov/stats/reports/diversitylaw/index.html.

40. W. L. Duvall, "Cardiovascular Disease in Women," *Mt. Sinai Journal of Medicine,* October 2003, pp. 293–305.

41. Jennifer Steinhauer, "For Women in Medicine, a Road to Compromise, Not Perks," *New York Times,* March 1, 1999.

CHAPTER 7
SECOND CHANCES FOR MOTHERS ON THE FAST TRACK

1. http://ucfamilyedge.berkeley.edu/ucfamilyfriendlyedge.html.
2. Molly Moore, "As Europe Grows Grayer, France Devises a Baby Boom," *Washington Post,* October 18, 2006, p. A1.
3. Claudia Dreifus, "Solving a Mystery of Life, Then Tackling a Real-Life Problem," *New York Times,* July 4, 2006.
4. Dreifus, "Solving a Mystery."
5. Deborah Rhode, *Unfinished Agenda: Women and the Legal Profession,* ABA Report, 2001, p. 33; Women's Bar Association of Massachusetts, *More Than Part-Time: The Effect of Reduced Hours on the Retention, Recruitment, and Success of Women Attorneys in Law Firms,* 2000.
6. Project for Attorney Retention, *Balanced Hours: Effective Part-Time Policies for Washington Law Firms,* www.pardc.org/Publications/BalancedHours_sum.shtml.
7. Project for Attorney Retention, *Balanced Hours.*
8. PARS, *Better on Balance? The Corporate Counsel Work/Life Report,* December 2003, 24.
9. Sylvia Ann Hewlett and Carolyn Buck Luce, "Off Ramps and On Ramps: Keeping Talented Women on the Road to Success," *Harvard Business Review* 9416 (2005).
10. Council on Contemporary Families, *Housework, Parental Leave, Family Benefits, and Childcare in Perspective: Family Policies in the US, France, Germany, Italy, and Japan,* www.contemporaryfamilies.org/Int%27l%20Family%20Policy.htm.
11. Council on Contemporary Families, *Housework.*
12. Hewlett and Luce, "Off Ramps and On Ramps."
13. Hewlett and Luce, "Off Ramps and On Ramps."
14. Mary Ann Mason and Marc Goulden, "Do Babies Matter? The Effect of Family Formation on the Lifelong Careers of Academic Men and Women," *Academe,* November–December 2002, pp. 21–27.

INDEX